The Authors   CARRIE FORMAN ARNOLD is an artist and businesswoman who has made a study of the history of the Palace of the Governors.

ADRIAN H. BUSTAMANTE is an ethnohistorian and head of the Arts and Sciences Division a the Santa Fe Community College.

STANLEY M. HORDES, an anthropologist and historian, was formerly the New Mexico state historian.

JOHN L. KESSELL, professor of history and editor of the Vargas Project at the University of New Mexico, is the author of *Kiva, Cross, and Crown: The Pecos Indians and New Mexico, 1540–1840.*

JANET LECOMPTE, a historian, is the author of *Rebellion in Rio Arriba, 1837,* and of seve articles on republican New Mexico.

FRANCES LEVINE is an ethnohistorian specializing in Spanish Colonial New Mexico.

DAVID GRANT NOBLE is an author, editor, and photographer and director of public information at the School of American Research.

JOSEPH P. SÁNCHEZ, a historian and the director of the Spanish Colonial Research Center a the University of New Mexico, is the author of *The Rio Abajo Frontier, 1540–1692: A History of Early Colonial New Mexico.*

MARC SIMMONS, a historian specializing in New Mexico and the Southwest, is the author of *Along the Santa Fe Trail, New Mexico: An Interpretive History,* and many other book and articles.

JOHN P. WILSON is an anthropologist who currently runs a business specializing in innovat historical and anthropological research.

SANTA FE

History of an Ancient City

The School of American Research
wishes to thank the
Kirkpatrick family and the Inn at Loretto in Santa Fe
for their generous support of this book

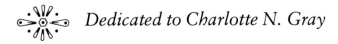 *Dedicated to Charlotte N. Gray*

SANTA FE

History of an Ancient City

Edited by

DAVID GRANT NOBLE

School of American Research Press

SCHOOL OF AMERICAN RESEARCH PRESS
P.O. Box 2188, Santa Fe, New Mexico 87504

Assistant editor: Tom Ireland
Designer: Deborah Flynn Post
Typographer: Casa Sin Nombre
Printer: Dai Nippon Printing Co.

DISTRIBUTED BY UNIVERSITY OF WASHINGTON PRESS

Library of Congress Cataloging-in-Publication Data:

Santa Fe: history of an ancient city
edited by David Grant Noble

p.   cm.   Bibliography: p.   Includes index.
ISBN 0-933452-26-8. -- ISBN 0-933452-27-6 (pbk.)
1. Santa Fe (N.M.)--History.   I. Noble, David Grant.
F804.S257S26   1989
978.9'5602--dc19   89-4214
CIP

Front cover: "The End of the Trail," oil painting by Gerald Cassidy, 48" x
60," ca. 1930. Courtesy Fine Arts Museum, Museum of New Mexico.
Frontispiece: Palace of the Governors, ca. 1900. Photo by
Christian G. Kaadt. Courtesy Carrie Forman Arnold.

Contents

Acknowledgments

The School of American Research is grateful to
the following people for their assistance and
support of this book: Margaret Arrott,
Renee and John Benjamin, Charles Bennett,
Nancy Bernard, Tom Chavez, Robin Farwell Gavin,
Charlotte N. Gray, Peggy Grinnell, Roy Grinnell,
Jonathan Haas, Laura Holt, Stanley M. Hordes,
Wilson Hurley, Paul Andrew Hutton,
Byron A. Johnson, James F. Kirkpatrick,
Lester B. Loo, Timothy D. Maxwell,
Barbara Mauldin, Arthur Olivas,
A. Lincoln Pittinger, Stephen S. Post,
Orlando Romero, Richard Rudisill,
James Russell, Curtis Schaafsma,
Albert and Barbara Simms, Cordelia Snow,
David Snow, Don Spalding, Louise Steiner,
Rosemary Talley, Charles Venrick,
and Samantha Williams.

We would also like to express our
appreciation to the following institutions for
their assistance: the Albuquerque Museum; the
Museum of New Mexico's Fine Arts Museum,
Laboratory of Anthropology, Museum of
International Folk Art, Palace of the Governors,
and Photo Archives; the New Mexico
Records Center and Archives; and Sunwest Bank
of Santa Fe.

Foreword

When I moved to Santa Fe in the early 1970s, my neighbor told me of her childhood, when she and her family followed the winding trail up Santa Fe Canyon to the mountain meadows of Aspen Ranch. Here they summered, grazing their goats and returning only occasionally to town to sell the cheese they made.

Oral history, which recalls the events of a lifetime and recounts the collective memory of several more, gives us an intimate and often colorful sense of where we live and the generations that preceded us. Old timers in Santa Fe tell of the burros that brought firewood to town from the surrounding hills. And they remember when you could build a house for "ten dollars a thousand, made and laid"—ten dollars to have a thousand adobe bricks made and laid up in the walls.

But it is equally fascinating to take the longer view of the past, the perspective of centuries surviving in the papers of officialdom, church documents, the journals and chronicles of the major players, and the archaeological record. Here the sweep of centuries supersedes the passage of mere generations.

The earliest era of Santa Fe history is difficult to resurrect because warfare, which swept through New Mexico in 1680, destroyed all local documents and erased most traces of Spanish settlement and culture. Today, historians regularly travel to Mexico City and Seville in their attempts to reconstruct the life and times of seventeenth-century Santa Fe and New Mexico.

One intriguing question that may never be fully answered is exactly how the site for Santa Fe was chosen in 1609 by Don Pedro de Peralta. In 1598, Don Juan de Oñate had settled his colonists at San Juan Pueblo along the Rio Chama, later moving to nearby Yunge Oweenge, which the Spaniards called San Gabriel. Unlike these first locations, the site along the Rio Santa Fe was not occupied by Native Americans. After twelve years of close interaction with and dependency upon Pueblo Indians, the Spaniards may have needed the independence that the Santa Fe site offered.

San Miguel Church, 1873.

But certainly other factors were taken into account. Peralta's people needed a reliable water supply and a topography allowing irrigation. They also required good land to farm, meadows in which to graze their stock and grow hay, a supply of wood for fuel and construction, and nearby areas offering hunting and other resources. And finally, the site would have to provide security from potential attack. Santa Fe seemed to satisfy all these requirements.

In the nearly four centuries since Peralta and his company surveyed the site for Santa Fe, the town has been ruled by Spaniards, Pueblo Indians, Mexicans, and Americans. For many generations, its basically rural character was complemented by the energy of a political center and military headquarters. Later, Santa Fe thrived as a marketplace and thoroughfare for international trade. The city has seen its measure of history.

Today, Santa Fe's historical ambiance draws visitors from around the country and abroad. The city's history is no less than an economic resource from which spring the livelihoods of many people. Indeed, "Santa Fe style" has become a small national industry. Like past travelers who came over the Camino Real or the Santa Fe Trail, today's visitors come with a stirring image of the city. This image has been created, although with some romantic embellishments, from a truly intriguing past.

As we approach Santa Fe's four hundredth anniversary, we would do well to look closely at the city's historical foundation and reappraise its value from various perspectives—educational, scholarly, artistic, economic. Are we adequately nurturing Santa Fe's history? Are archaeological sites being responsibly investigated and interpreted? Do our history libraries need support? How much do our students know about their ethnic past? Is scholarly research being encouraged? Does the city adequately protect architectural integrity? How will the next generation of tourists respond to the Santa Fe they will experience? Santa Fe's history supports Santa Fe, but does Santa Fe support its history?

Some four centuries ago, Governor Peralta selected a site along the Santa Fe River for the establishment of his colony. Although we have no record of his thoughts, we can assume that he carefully considered how the place would serve the needs of his followers. He probably walked along the banks of the river, tasted the water, tested the soil, and explored the foothills. Certainly, he prepared for the oncoming winter and planned for the following spring. And he must have pondered the fate of the future generations he would not see. Perhaps his faith in the site inspired the name he gave it, *Santa Fe*, Holy Faith.

Four centuries later, as we ourselves look to Santa Fe's future, we can benefit by knowing its past and by assessing, as did Peralta, the resources that future generations will need to thrive. Santa Fe's historical heritage should be counted among them; like the city's precious water supply, it must be both used and conserved.

It is my hope that the present essays, which represent the latest thinking of some of New Mexico's most distinguished historians, will help deepen public understanding and appreciation of Santa Fe's fascinating past and stimulate wise planning for its future.

David Grant Noble

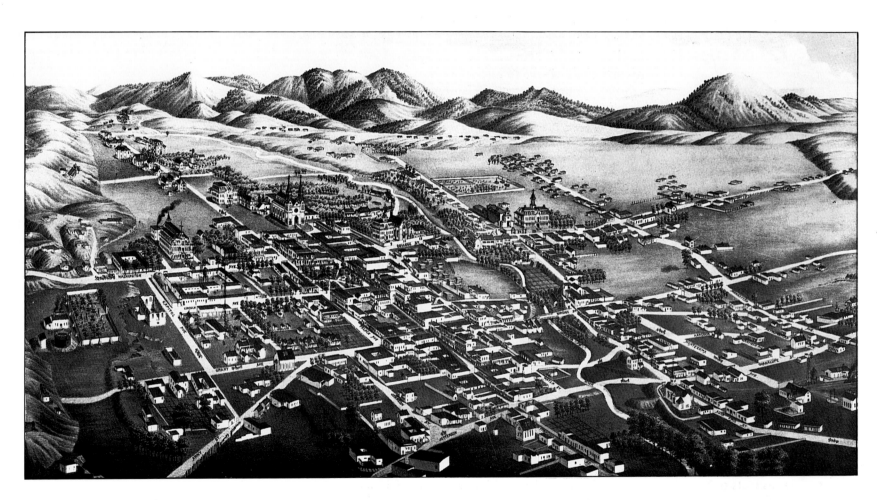

Bird's-eye view of Santa Fe in 1882.

Introduction:

A History of the History of Santa Fe*

STANLEY M. HORDES

One could scarcely imagine a town more deserving of a historical volume than Santa Fe. Established in 1610, it stands as the oldest capital city in what is now the United States. For almost two and a half centuries, it represented the administrative, military, and commercial center of the Spanish and Mexican far northern frontier—first as the terminus of the Camino Real, or Royal Highway, which stretched over one thousand miles from the viceregal capital in Mexico City, and later as the destination of Anglo traders carrying goods from the United States along the Santa Fe Trail. Even today, Santa Fe maintains an international reputation as a historically significant city, whether based on its rich architectural and archaeological resources or on its "Pueblo Revival" buildings.

This volume draws together the talents of a distinguished group of New Mexico historians to examine the history of Santa Fe from a variety of fresh scholarly perspectives, ranging from the occupation of the area by prehistoric Indian groups, through the Spanish and Mexican periods, to the early years of occupation by the United States. Indeed, the collective efforts of these scholars fill a large void in the historical literature on the city's heritage. Until recently, only two attempts have been made to offer a comprehensive historical account, one by Ralph Emerson Twitchell in 1925, and the other by Father Stanley Cracciola in 1958, both inadequate by today's standards. The remainder of the works consist of a few monographs and journal articles on various aspects of Santa Fe's history. These tend to fall into three general categories: descriptions and translations of documents; arguments over dates of

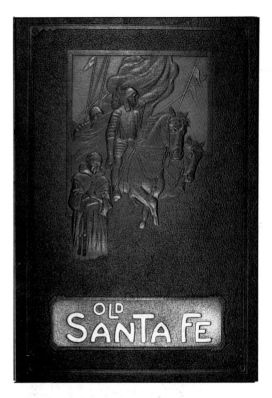

Old Santa Fe: The Story of New Mexico's Ancient Capital, by Ralph Emerson Twitchell.

buildings or events; and site-specific studies, more often than not, prepared in response to physical threats to the resource.

Twitchell's *Old Santa Fe: The Story of New Mexico's Ancient Capital* (1925) represented a noble effort on the part of the prolific lawyer / historian to piece together a chronicle of the city from its origins until the early years of the twentieth century. While this work must be respected as a pioneering attempt and remains the most utilized book on the topic, it has its share of problems, including an anecdotal narrative style, significant chronological gaps, and the absence of Hispanic figures in its treatment of the Territorial period. Less satisfying still is Father Stanley Cracciola's *Ciudad Santa Fe* (1958), a long, rambling essay that includes very little material on Santa Fe itself, concentrating on New Mexico history in general. Moreover, Father Stanley maintained a strongly anti-Hispanic bias in his approach to history, leading the reader to conclude incorrectly that the Spaniards came to New Mexico exclusively to rape and pillage.

Fortunately, Susan Hazen-Hammond's *A Short History of Santa Fe* (1988) offered an excellent synthesis of both the classical authors and more recent research, recounting Santa Fe's past from prehistory to the present. As it was based almost entirely on secondary works and edited translations of original documents, the work broke little new ground, and to a certain extent, it perpetuated the perspectives of its sources. But for the first time, the reader can benefit from scholarship produced during the mid and late twentieth century.

Several monographs and journal articles published over the course of the past sixty years shed considerable light on Santa Fe's past. Two journals in particular—*El Palacio* (published jointly by the School of American Research, the Museum of New Mexico, and the Archaeological Society of New Mexico until the 1950s) and the *New Mexico Historical Review*—have taken the lead in this direction. In the 1920s, Lansing Bloom started the tradition of publishing annotated translations of significant documents illustrating key historical developments in the history of Santa Fe. His article on the trading activities of Mexican-period merchant Manuel Alvarez (*El Palacio*, 1923) and his translation of the royal instructions to Governor Pedro de Peralta in 1609 regarding the establishment of the capital at Santa Fe (*El Palacio*, 1928) established the precedent for later scholars to share their newly discovered documents with the public—for example, Marc Simmons's translation of "Antonio Barreiro's Proclamation of Santa Fe City Government" (*El Palacio*, 1970) and Clevy Lloyd Strout's "The Resettlement of Santa Fe, 1695: The Newly Found Muster Roll" (*New Mexico Historical Review*, 1978).

A considerable share of the articles written about Santa Fe in the early part of the twentieth century tended to focus on the dating of particular buildings and events or the city's name. In a protracted debate, Benjamin M. Read claimed that Juan de Oñate established Santa Fe as the capital of New Mexico ("The Founder of Santa Fe," *El Palacio*, 1927), and Lansing Bloom contended (correctly) that Pedro de Peralta did ("Instructions for Don Pedro de Peralta . . . in the Place of Don Juan de Oñate," *El Palacio*, 1928; "When Was Santa Fe Founded?" *New Mexico Historical Review*, 1929). Bloom also tackled the controversial issue of the name of Santa Fe, favoring "La Villa de Santa Fe" over the more romantic and flowery "La Villa Real de la Santa Fe de San Francisco de Asis," which is still the official name according to the city ("What is Santa Fe's Name Historically?" *New Mexico Historical Review*, 1945). Still other articles dealt with the age of San Miguel Chapel, which some people claim to be the oldest church in the United States (e.g., Fray Angelico Chávez, "How Old is San Miguel?" *El Palacio*, 1953).

The recognition of the need to protect and interpret Santa Fe's architectural and archaeological treasures stimulated another genre of historical scholarship. Beginning in the 1930s and continuing through the 1980s, historians and archaeologists documented significant buildings and sites in downtown Santa Fe. The city's churches attracted the attention of most of these writers, led by historian Fray Angelico Chávez, whose many articles in the *New Mexico Historical Review* in the 1940s, 1950s, and 1960s shed new light on Santa Fe's past. Among others instrumental in documenting the history of these structures were Eleanor Adams (with Chávez, the coauthor of *The Missions of New Mexico, 1776*), A. von Wuthenau, José D. Sena, and Bruce Ellis. Of particular value is Mary Jean Straw's *Loretto: The Sisters and Their Santa Fe*

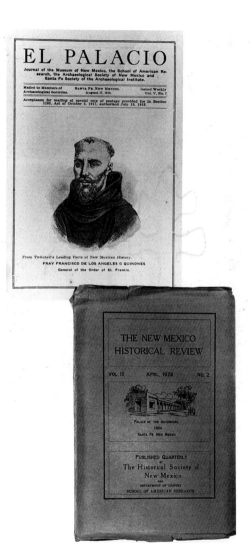

Early issues of *El Palacio* and the *New Mexico Historical Review.*

Double-barred cross
excavated from the Palace of
the Governors.

Chapel, which went considerably beyond a mere building history to encompass the people associated with the structure.

For many years, threats from intrusive development have stimulated studies of Santa Fe's built environment. As long ago as the 1920s, Twitchell wrote a short essay, *The Conquest of Santa Fe, New Mexico, and the Building of Old Fort Marcy,* A.D. *1846,* to generate interest in the restoration of the old fort. Civic organizations formed to protect the architectural heritage of Santa Fe, such as the Old Santa Fe Association (1926) and the Historic Santa Fe Foundation (1961), supported historical research on structures throughout the city. The two groups sponsored a series of essays in the *New Mexican* entitled "Let's Keep Our Heritage," edited by architect John Gaw Meem, and in 1966 published *Old Santa Fe Today* (republished in 1972 and 1982), containing architectural histories of significant buildings in Santa Fe and biographical sketches of their former occupants. With new threats of instrusive development in the 1970s and 1980s came a renewed interest in the underground resources of Santa Fe and their historical contexts. *El Palacio* featured the work of Cordelia Snow, Bruce Ellis, David Snow, Stewart Peckham, and Curtis Schaafsma, writing about their excavations at the Palace of the Governors, the Museum of Fine Arts, Nusbaum House, and La Garita (see bibiliography).

Not surprisingly, the plaza and its surrounding buildings have attracted a large share of scholarly attention. Bruce Ellis's "Santa Fe's Seventeenth Century Plaza, Parish Church, and Convent Reconsidered" (1976), Max Moorehead's "Rebuilding the Presidio of Santa Fe, 1789-1791" (*New Mexico Historical Review,* 1974), and J. K. Shishkin's *The Palace of the Governors* (1972) are but a few of these studies.

This brief review of the scholarship dealing with the history of Santa Fe suggests that with few exceptions the literature has been either too broad, treating the larger unit of New Mexico and neglecting the history of the city, or too narrow, focusing on site-specific topics to the exclusion of the larger municipal context. Although the Hazen-Hammond history partially fills this void, a considerable amount of archival material remains untouched.

Much significant material may be found in repositories such as the Archivo General de Indias in Seville, the Archivo Histórico Nacional in Madrid, the Archivo General de la Nación and the Biblioteca Nacional in Mexico City, and various regional archives in northern Mexico. But the richest sources exist in local archives and libraries, most notably at the New Mexico Records Center and Archives and the Museum of New Mexico History Library. Contained among these tens of thousands of pages of official and private papers are administrative, judicial, military, and church records documenting the activities not only of the movers and shakers of the community, but also of the more humble residents of Santa Fe. By examining civil proceedings and land records, for example, one can begin to discern patterns of urban and rural land ownership in the area—who was accumulating wealth and power at whose expense. By analyzing criminal trials, scholars can begin to better understand standards of behavior and morality during the Spanish and Mexican periods of Santa Fe's history. Church baptismal, marriage, and burial records, together with civil and ecclesiastical census records, can yield a considerable amount of information on Santa Fe's changing demographic profile in the seventeenth, eighteenth, and nineteenth centuries.

South side of the Santa Fe plaza.

The articles assembled in this volume are an example of the level of research and analysis that can be achieved when scholars cultivate the fertile fields of Santa Fe history. Frances Levine offers an overview of prehistoric and historic archaeological resources in the Santa Fe area, analyzing the cultural chronology revealed by these resources and reviewing efforts to interpret their significance. Joseph P. Sánchez, director of the National Park Service's Spanish Colonial Research Center at the University of New Mexico, tells how a struggle between civil and ecclesiastical authorities in the seventeenth century influenced life in the young Spanish capital and details the harrowing events of the Pueblo Revolt of 1680. The story of the reconquest of Santa Fe thirteen years later is recounted by University of New Mexico Professor John L. Kessell, and Adrian Bustamante, of Santa Fe Community College, examines the ethnic and social diversity of the city in Spanish Colonial times.

Janet Lecompte, Marc Simmons, and John P. Wilson investigate the Mexican period of Santa Fe's history. Lecompte discusses the changing lifestyle of Santa Feans in the wake of Mexican independence from Spain in 1821 and the influx of Anglo-Americans brought about by the opening of the Santa Fe Trail. The trail is the focus of Simmons's article, which analyzes the interdependent roles of Anglo and Mexican merchants and the impact of their relationship on the community. Wilson recounts the invasion and occupation of Santa Fe in 1846 by General Stephen Watts Kearny and fifteen hundred U.S. troops, ending nearly two and a half centuries of Spanish and Mexican administration and causing dramatic changes in the lives of Santa Fe's residents.

Encompassing all periods of Santa Fe's history, Carrie Forman Arnold traces the evolution of the Palace of the Governors from its construction in 1610 to its most recent renovation in the 1980s. The *casas reales*, or *palacio real*, as the structure was once known, represents Santa Fe's transition over the course of four centuries—the architectural manifestation of its transformation from frontier backwater capital to tourist mecca.

The history of Santa Fe is reflected in the wealth of architectural, archaeological, and documentary resources of the community. The scholars whose work is represented in this volume have gone a long way towards realizing the tremendous research potential of these precious resources. It is hoped that the scholarship presented here will serve not only to enlighten the community about its past but also to stimulate other researchers to delve into primary archival materials with the end of better understanding Santa Fe's unique heritage.

---

* No attempt is made here to examine the general literature treating the history of New Mexico, although the author realizes that many such works include significant material on the history of Santa Fe.

A Short Chronology of Santa Fe

Ca. 1150–1325	Coalition period. Pueblo Indian villages thrive along the Santa Fe River.
Ca. 1325–1600	Classic period. Indians abandon the area by the early 1400s.
1598	Establishment of the first permanent Spanish colony in New Mexico at San Juan Pueblo.
1610	Founding of Santa Fe by Spaniards. The building of the Palace of the Governors begins.
1680	Pueblo Revolt. Spanish colony exiled.
1693	Santa Fe reconquered by Spaniards under Vargas.
1821	Mexico wins independence from Spain. Santa Fe Trail opens.
1846	Conquest of Santa Fe and New Mexico by the United States.
1880	Railway reaches Santa Fe. The end of commerce on the Santa Fe Trail.
1912	New Mexico achieves statehood.

Interior of Loretto Chapel showing spiral staircase, ca. 1935.

Down Under an Ancient City

An Archaeologist's View of Santa Fe

FRANCES LEVINE

Santa Fe recently commemorated its three hundred seventy-fifth year as the capital of New Mexico and its proud heritage as one of the oldest cities in the nation. But Santa Fe has an even longer legacy. Scattered throughout the city are archaeological remains of Pueblo Indian villages that were occupied over a span of more than seven centuries.

Between about A.D. 600 and 1425, ancestors of the modern Pueblos lived along the Santa Fe River. Why did they abandon the area that Spanish colonists later found so attractive for their capital city? In part, rainfall in the early fifteenth century may have been insufficient to support the farming communities in and around Santa Fe. We do not yet fully understand the reasons for this abandonment because the archaeological resources of Santa Fe have not been as systematically studied as those of many other parts of the Southwest. Yet the archeological remains of the Pueblo, Hispanic, and Anglo-American occupations of Santa Fe contain evidence of a fascinating and largely untold history of "the City Different."

Prehistoric Cultures of the Northern Rio Grande

The city of Santa Fe lies within the northern Rio Grande region. Archaeological remains of hunting camps and temporary shelters containing stone tools and utilitarian and crudely painted pottery are evidence of the mobile life-style of the Archaic people who lived in the region between about 3000 B.C. and A.D. 600. They lived in small, probably family-based bands, scheduling their frequent moves by the seasonal and local availability of edible wild plants and

Above, Red Mesa bowl. *Opposite page*, archaeological excavations at the building site of the First Interstate Bank on Washington Avenue in 1982.

Archaic campsite.

Santa Fe Black-on-white mug.

game. Archaic sites have not yet been recorded closer to Santa Fe than the Cochiti area, some twenty-five miles southwest of the city.

Beginning perhaps in the fifth century A.D. and certainly by the beginning of the seventh century, people in the northern Rio Grande began to shift their economy from foraging to farming. For some five hundred years, beginning about A.D. 400–600 and lasting until A.D. 1150–1200, these early agriculturalists lived in small villages of pithouses or in surface masonry houses. Red Mesa Black-on-white, Kwahe'e Black-on-white, and Chaco II Black-on-white—geometrically patterned, mineral-painted pottery styles—characterize archaeological sites of this so-called Developmental period. Some pottery was produced in the Santa Fe villages, but several kinds of ceramics seem to have been traded into this area from pueblos further to the west, perhaps from the flourishing cultural center of Chaco Canyon.

Few Early Developmental sites have been found in the northern Rio Grande, which suggests that the population was small, or perhaps that this area was not favorable for incipient agricultural practices. Sites of the Late Developmental period are more abundant.

As the Developmental period drew to a close, the population of the northern Rio Grande was expanding, using the major river valleys for villages and fields and the nearby mountains for game and wild plant foods. By the mid-twelfth century, a virtual population explosion had taken place in the northern Rio Grande. Archaeologists traditionally have attributed the growth to an immigration of people from the Mesa Verde area, Chaco Canyon, and the San Juan Basin of northwestern New Mexico, believing that people left those areas as the climatic and cultural conditions changed. Other evidence suggests that the local population may have been large enough by the mid-twelfth century to require new agricultural technology, economic practices, and settlement patterns.

Archaeological remains of the Coalition period, which began between A.D. 1150 and 1200 and ended at about A.D. 1325, are found widely throughout the northern Rio Grande. Coalition-period sites underlie parts of downtown Santa Fe and are found in the nearby settlements of Agua Fria and

Arroyo Hondo. During this period pottery production underwent a series of technological changes, and the inhabitants began to settle in fewer and larger villages. Archaeological sites of this age are identified by the prevalence of a locally made vegetable- or organic-painted pottery called Santa Fe Black-on-white and by the presence of a later variant known as Wiyo Black-on-white. Coalition architecture is variable, but most villages have multiroom masonry or adobe houseblocks built around plazas and include characteristic round, subterranean kivas.

The transition from the Coalition to the Classic period (A.D. 1325–1600) is identified archaeologically by the appearance of pottery decorated with mineral-paint glazes and by a thick, porous pottery known as biscuit ware. Early in the Classic period, population seems to have increased, as evidenced by more and larger villages. Classic-period settlements are frequently associated with soil- and water-conservation features such as check dams and gridded gardens, indicating the extent to which the population was committed to farming. The appearance of kachina figures in rock art and ritual paraphernalia and the common occurrence of great kivas in Classic-period sites suggest that Pueblo society had complex regional social and political organizations. Village craft specialization also flourished during this period. Pottery styles produced in a number of the northern Rio Grande pueblos are found in archaeological sites throughout the Southwest and High Plains, indicating that some pueblos in the northern Rio Grande supplied goods to regional trade networks.

The Early Classic period seems to mark the end of Pueblo occupation in Santa Fe, Agua Fria, and Arroyo Hondo, although there was a brief interval of Pueblo reoccupation of Santa Fe following the Pueblo Revolt of 1680. In other parts of the northern Rio Grande, Classic-period archaeological sites, including the Tano pueblos of the Galisteo Basin, Tesuque Pueblo, and Pecos Pueblo, were still occupied at the time of Spanish contact.

Toward the end of the Classic period and continuing into the seventeenth century, the population of the northern Rio Grande pueblos declined dramatically. Diseases introduced by the Spaniards decimated the Pueblos. A collapse of the aboriginal social and economic networks accompanied this

Wijo canteen.

Kachina mask petroglyph south of Santa Fe, thought to represent Hilili, the guardian kachina.

decline, leading to the abandonment of some villages and the concentration of population into others. Santa Fe was not one of the areas in which the Pueblo population concentrated. It would be more than two and a half centuries before Pueblo people again occupied Santa Fe, and then, their brief occupation was abruptly terminated when they were removed by Spanish troops.

Archaeological Investigations in Santa Fe

Archaeological studies along the Santa Fe River began in the late nineteenth century. During the 1880s, Adolph Bandelier, the father of southwestern archaeology and ethnology, recorded a number of late prehistoric and historic pueblos in Santa Fe County in his attempts to find the ancestral sites of the modern pueblos of the Rio Grande. He speculated that Santa Fe had been the site of one or two Tano-speaking villages related linguistically to the pueblos of the Galisteo area. He believed that the Tanos abandoned Santa Fe at least a century before the establishment of the Spanish capital in 1610. Bandelier placed one of the Tano pueblos in Santa Fe north of the city, near the later site of Fort Marcy. The other, he thought, had stood in the vicinity of San Miguel Church. Bandelier's Tewa-speaking informants from San Juan and Santa Clara pueblos called Santa Fe Kua'p'o-oge or O'gha po'oghe, meaning "the place of the shell beads near the water," or "bead water place."

In June of 1910, a skeleton was unearthed during construction of the Sylvanus Morley house on La Garita Hill, the area east of the Scottish Rite Temple bordered by Paseo de Peralta on the south and Washington Avenue on the west. Edgar Hewett, then director of the School of American Archaeology (later the School of American Research), used the occasion to prepare a brief review of the prehistory of Santa Fe for the *New Mexican*. Hewett believed that there were three pueblo ruins in the city—one underlying the ruins of Fort Marcy, a smaller one near San Miguel Chapel and a downtown tourist attraction that is touted as the "oldest house" in the continental United States, and a third underlying the Palace of the Governors. He vividly rendered the landscape of fifteenth-century Santa Fe as follows:

Adolph F. Bandelier at an archaeological ruin.

If one could have stood on the spot where the city now stands, looking east from the site of the Church of Our Lady of Guadalupe, five hundred years ago, there would have been seen on what we call Fort Marcy hill, an Indian town of considerable size, consisting of one large terraced pueblo and one or two smaller buildings near by, a kiva or sanctuary of the circular, subterranean type on the bench half way down the hill side; south of the river on San Miguel slope, a small pueblo two stories high, and passing back and forth from these two towns to the river, then considerably larger than now, the water carriers with their ollas on their heads. In the foreground, where the historic Old Palace has undergone the vicissitudes of nearly three centuries, would have been a cluster of ruined walls and rounded mounds, the remains of an earlier town, over which some of the earliest houses of Santa Fe were doubtless built.

Edgar Lee Hewett, 1911.

Some months after Hewett's published description, the historian Ralph Emerson Twitchell responded in another *New Mexican* column, stating that no pueblo existed in the vicinity of San Miguel Church, although the "oldest house" was probably of Pueblo construction. Twitchell believed that the other Pueblo ruins in Santa Fe were attributable to Tano-speaking peoples. The debate between Hewett and Twitchell makes interesting reading, but their disagreements are largely moot. With more precise dating of archaeological remains, it is now clear that the population of Santa Fe was declining in the fifteenth century, and it is unlikely that the pueblos were as bustling as Hewett depicts. As for Twitchell's rejection of the idea of a pueblo near San Miguel Church, Coalition-period remains have been found under its earliest floor levels, underlying the PERA building, and in other construction sites east of the church.

The *New Mexican* contains the only record of archaeological materials removed during the 1916 demolition of the Fort Marcy barracks, which stood on the site now occupied by the Museum of Fine Arts. Wagon loads of Pueblo pottery and Spanish crockery, animal bones, assorted household and personal

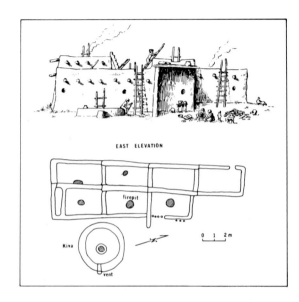

EAST ELEVATION

firepit

Kiva

vent

0 1 2m

Reconstruction of a Coalition pueblo.

items, and as many as six human burials were found in cultural deposits extending more than ten feet below the street level in some places.

The first three decades of the twentieth century were seminal years for the development of southwestern archaeological methods and theories. The School of American Research and the Laboratory of Anthropology provided intellectual and logistical support to a distinguished group of scholars who came to study the archaeology and ethnology of the northern Rio Grande. Edgar Hewett, Harry P. Mera, Nels Nelson, A. V. Kidder, Anna O. Shepard, Kenneth Chapman, and many others developed the systematic classifications of ceramics and the site-recording procedures that remain fundamental to archaeological studies in the region. The continuum of culture in the later prehistoric, historic, and modern pueblos of the northern Rio Grande provided archaeologists with the laboratory they needed to refine their techniques. Excavations in the Galisteo Basin pueblos, at Pecos, and at La Cieneguilla established the procedures for using specific pottery designs to date the occupation of archaeological sites.

In Santa Fe the most significant archaeological study of the 1930s was the excavation of Pindi, a Late Developmental- and Coalition-period site in Agua Fria. Laborers hired by the Works Progress Administration excavated the site, and Stanley Stubbs and W. S. Stallings documented the work. The site is one of the larger Coalition sites in the northern Rio Grande. Until recent studies by the School of American Research in the Arroyo Hondo area, this was the only comprehensive excavation and reporting of a prehistoric site in Santa Fe.

In the 1950s a number of projects in and near Santa Fe focused on the Spanish Colonial archaeology of the city. Stubbs and Bruce Ellis excavated within the sanctuary of San Miguel Chapel to reconstruct the building sequence of the church. They also excavated what remained of La Castrense, the eighteeenth-century chapel that had stood on the south side of the plaza. During this time Ellis also excavated the architectural remains of La Garita, a Colonial fortification on the north side of the city. Also beginning in the 1950s, a study of Spanish Colonial and Mexican-period ranchos in the area between Cieneguilla and Agua Fria was carried out by E. Boyd over a period of some

Archaeological excavations at Pindi Pueblo showing outlines of turkey pens under the plaza. Pindi is located along the Santa Fe River west of downtown Santa Fe.

twenty years. Boyd, then curator of Spanish Colonial art at the Museum of International Folk Art of the Museum of New Mexico, performed limited test excavations at these sites to examine the range of Hispanic domestic artifacts.

Since the early 1970s, the number of archaeological excavations in Santa Fe has increased. Downtown and suburban development has been responsible for much of this research. Unfortunately, few of the excavation projects have had the funds necessary to completely analyze the materials recovered from the sites or to report these finds.

Storage jars under excavation at the Pojoaque Grant site.

What was it about the location of Santa Fe that made it desirable to Pueblo Indians from the tenth to the fourteenth centuries and then, in the early decades of the fifteenth century, caused them to abandon their settlements here?

The initial Pueblo occupation in Santa Fe appears to date from the Late Developmental period. An early occupation level of Pindi Pueblo, on the west side of the Santa Fe River in Agua Fria; the Arroyo Negro site, in south Santa Fe; and a number of sites in the vicinity of Fort Marcy and the Hillside neighborhood have yielded evidence of Late Developmental pithouses and associated artifacts. The Arroyo Negro site covers an extensive area and may represent an important village of the mid-eleventh century.

Some of the most intriguing Developmental archaeological sites are located in the Tesuque and Cerrillos areas. The Pojoaque Grant site is an extensive settlement of small adobe and jacal houses and a great kiva located near the pueblos of Pojoaque and Tesuque. The site shows Chacoan influence in architecture and associated pottery types, traditionally attributed to migrants from Chaco Canyon who began to move into the Rio Grande area as cultural and environmental conditions in Chaco Canyon changed, and who may have occupied this settlement.

Recent work at the Bronze Trail site group, near Cerrillos, and intensive studies at Chaco Canyon have suggested alternative explanations for the apparent Chaco influences in the northern Rio Grande during the Developmental period. The Bronze Trail site group, the Pojoaque Grant site, and the Arroyo Negro site were occupied in the mid-eleventh century, when the influence of Chaco throughout the Southwest was at its greatest. All these sites contain pottery that was produced in the Chaco-Mount Taylor area or influenced by Chacoan ceramic designs. The Bronze Trail site group differs from the Pojoaque and Cerrillos sites in that it appears to lack houses and to have been used solely for mining and processing turquoise from the famous Cerrillos turquoise mines. Turquoise found in sites in the Mount Taylor area and in Chaco Canyon appears to come from the Cerrillos mines. It seems likely that the Chaco influence observed in northern Rio Grande Developmental sites is related to an exchange of Cerrillos turquoise for food or other natural resources, but the connection may have been ritual rather than material. With the limited evidence available, it can be argued either that Chaco migrants occupied these northern Rio Grande sites or that the local people were copying Chaco-like architectural details and pottery designs. Additional studies of Developmental sites in the Santa Fe area have much to contribute to our understanding of the complex social processes that were occurring throughout the Southwest in the tenth, eleventh, and twelfth centuries.

Coalition and Early Classic archaeological sites are the most impressive prehistoric resources in Santa Fe and the immediately adjacent villages. Pindi Pueblo, the adjacent Agua Fria School site, and Arroyo Hondo Pueblo are well-known Coalition sites in or near Santa Fe. Other archaeological remains from this period have been found in excavations in various parts of the city, including the vicinity of Fort Marcy and La Garita Hill and underlying the City Hall complex on Marcy Street.

Pindi is the Tewa word for turkey, so named for the abundance of turkey bones and droppings and the turkey-raising pens found during the excavation of the site. Pindi was constructed in at least three phases between about 1200 and 1350. Excavations revealed numerous rearrangments of the roomblocks, kivas, and outbuildings that constituted the Coalition-period occupation of the site; the final remodeling took place just before the abandonment of the site in 1350. Changes in ceramic technology seem to have accompanied many of the renovations of the site, perhaps indicating a period of intense economic or social change. Inhabitants of Pindi appear to have moved across the river to a pueblo now known as the School House site, where limited test excavations were conducted in 1988. The full extent and configuration of this prehistoric village are not yet known, but recovered potsherds point to possible relationships between the School House people and those living at other pueblos near Galisteo, Cieneguilla, and Arroyo Hondo. The pueblos of Pindi and School House may have been occupied contemporaneously in the mid-fourteenth century. Like Arroyo Hondo Pueblo, School House was abandoned in the early fifteenth century.

Cherie Scheick excavating a portion of the School House site, December 1988.

Ceremonial jar containing a shell necklace, excavated at Arroyo Hondo Pueblo in 1971.

Douglas W. Schwartz, 1972.

The School of American Research's Arroyo Hondo project, conducted in the 1970s under the direction of Douglas W. Schwartz, has provided stimulating information about past climate in the Santa Fe area and about the physical condition of the Pueblo population of Santa Fe in the fifteenth century. The pueblo of Arroyo Hondo was founded in about A.D. 1300, when the northern Rio Gránde population was settling into fewer, larger pueblos and beginning to use smaller tributary drainages of the Rio Grande proper. For about thirty years the village grew, and by about 1330 it had more than one thousand rooms in twenty-four houseblocks, surrounding ten plazas. Rainfall in the early fourteenth century was favorable to agriculture, native plant foods, and game. By 1335, however, Arroyo Hondo was in decline, and its Santa Fe contemporaries were also being abandoned. Much of Arroyo Hondo was dismantled systematically, and the entire site may have been abandoned for a time. The decline of the pueblo is dramatically visible in the high mortality rate among children under five and young adults, their skeletal remains clearly showing the ravages of malnutrition.

In the early 1370s, Arroyo Hondo began a second period of prosperity, and by 1400 or so the village consisted of nine roomblocks containing two hundred rooms, arranged around three plazas. This period of growth corresponds to another period of above-average rainfall. The second period of prosperity was over by 1410. A fire destroyed the pueblo in 1420. This event, coupled with a decimating drought between about 1415 and 1425, was no doubt responsible for the abandonment of Arroyo Hondo. Many other Classic sites in the northern Rio Grande were also abandoned at this time.

Historical Archaeology in Santa Fe

The Historic period in the northern Rio Grande is generally reckoned to begin with the contact between the Pueblos and the Vásquez de Coronado expedition of 1540; thus, the Historic period overlaps the end of the Classic period in the archaeological sequence. In Santa Fe, excavations of historic sites, largely occasioned by construction projects, are necessarily limited salvage

Aerial view of Arroyo Hondo Pueblo, 1971.

Objects excavated from the Palace of the Governors. *From left,* brass candle holder, unidentified, unidentified, double-barred cross, nail (?), needle.

Bandelier Black-on-cream jar.

projects. In most cases it has not been possible to recover more than a small fraction of the materials impacted by development.

The Santa Fe City Council recently passed an ordinance protecting archaeological resources within the city that are at least seventy-five years old. The council's unanimous vote of approval in the face of opposition from some developers was a significant gain for our community. Councilors and proponents who spoke in support of the ordinance emphasized the unique cultural history of Santa Fe and the importance of preserving the valuable information that has yet to be obtained from excavations in the city.

Historical archaeology has an important place in the history of Santa Fe. Much of our knowledge about seventeenth-century Santa Fe is drawn from eighteenth-century documents, earlier documentation having been destroyed during the Pueblo Revolt. Further, many aspects of daily life preserved in archival records are seldom recorded in official documents preserved in archives. The analysis of artifacts and food remains offers insight into Santa Fe's domestic life in much greater detail than is available from documentary sources alone. And when archaeological and historical investigations are combined, the details of daily life are placed in a larger cultural and historical context.

The plaza has been the central feature of European settlement in Santa Fe since 1610. Because of the longevity and intensity of land use around the plaza and as far north as the municipal office complex on Marcy Street, in some places more than ten feet of cultural stratigraphy underlie the street level. Within these deposits, which consist of structural debris, the bones of butchered animals, Puebloan pottery, and historic artifacts, exists a record of changes in diet, trade networks, and cultural practices during the course of Hispanic colonial and Anglo-American settlement.

In what is now the southwest corner of the patio of the Palace of the Governors, the Museum of New Mexico has reconstructed a well excavated by Marjorie Lambert in 1956. Lambert had hoped to be able to excavate a feature in the east part of the patio that she suspected was a domestic well dug some time around 1715. Museum officials were afraid that the well, described in colonial documents as 4 varas (about 11 feet) wide by 40 varas (almost 110 feet)

Marjorie F. Lambert and Bernie Valdez excavating well in the patio of the palace, 1956.

deep, would, if opened, pose a hazard to visitors. Instead, they allowed Lambert to excavate a well in the southwest corner. The nails, bottles, and horseshoes recovered date the use of this well to the mid to late nineteenth century.

Archaeologists and historians have varied opinions about the size and extent of the seventeenth- and eighteenth-century plaza area. Some authors have suggested that it was twice as long, east to west, and twice as wide, north to south, as it is now. A number of excavations in the downtown area have offered evidence in support of or in opposition to this suggestion.

Excavations in the block now occupied by the First Interstate Bank building, between Washington and Lincoln avenues to the north of the Palace of the Governors, produced evidence of more than two hundred years of occupation in deposits less than four feet below the street level. At the lowest level of this excavation, archaeologists found eighteenth-century Pueblo pottery and deposits that seem to correlate with the mid-1760s location of gardens and corrals shown on a 1766-1768 map of Santa Fe by Joseph de Urrutia. Foundations of what may have been part of the 1791 presidio overlay the deposits. These walls were later incorporated into structures used for the commissary, carpenter's shop, and smithy of Fort Marcy. Ruins of Fort Marcy and underlying Spanish Colonial foundations were also found during the 1979 excavations of the addition to the Fine Arts Museum.

Test excavations in the Water Street parking lot failed to find any evidence that structures were built in this area until the late 1800s. The majority of the artifacts and architectural features revealed by the excavations showed that this property was used primarily for industrial purposes. Between 1882 and 1887, a lumber company occupied the site. From 1891 to the mid-1960s, Public Service Company of New Mexico had a power generating station on the property. The small number of Spanish Colonial artifacts and the absence of structural remains indicates that the project area was not a residential property in the seventeenth or eighteenth centuries, but farm land, as shown on the Urrutia map.

This excavation and one in the parking lot between Saint Francis Cathedral and La Fonda offer additional perspectives on the extent of the plaza in the Colonial period. The absence of substantial Colonial deposits in the Water Street excavations suggests that the plaza did not extend that far south. The presence of a deep deposit of Spanish Colonial trash in excavations in the La Fonda parking lot confirms that the plaza did extend at least as far as the cathedral. The excavations at La Fonda were not extensive enough, however, to determine whether this deposit was associated with Colonial houses, corrals, or garden areas. Neither excavation found evidence of the *muralla*, or wall, which some authors speculate was built around the plaza by Spanish colonists before or after the Pueblo Revolt or by the Pueblo Indians who occupied the plaza area before the Reconquest (1680–1696). This may support the argument made by others that only the *casas reales*, or the immediate vicinity of the palace, was walled.

The Palace of the Governors has had a complex history, as revealed by archaeological studies that have accompanied many of the renovations to this

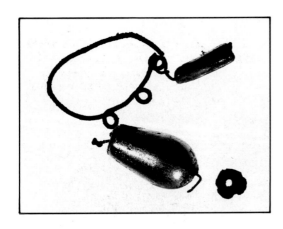

Earring excavated from the Palace of the Governors.

structure. Elsewhere in this volume, Carrie Forman Arnold traces its construction history. The excavations have yielded small amounts of jewelry, household objects of Spanish manufacture, and some personal items, but the bulk of material excavated has been comprised of animal bones, Puebloan pottery, and colorful Mexican majolica ceramics. Even within the palace, where one might expect to find evidence of how the wealthier residents of colonial Santa Fe lived, there is evidence of a rather Spartan life-style.

The plaza and the palace were not the only area of Spanish Colonial settlement. The ruins of La Garita, the Spanish Colonial fort built on the hill east of the Scottish Rite Temple, was once an important landmark in the folklore of Santa Fe. The ruins of the two adobe bastions of the fort were clearly visible as late as the 1920s. In 1954, portions of the little fortress-like structure were excavated by Bruce Ellis. The stone foundations showed that it was square, with pentagonal bastions on the northern and southern corners. At least three floor levels were revealed. Five pieces of rotted ponderosa pine were found, and tree-ring analysis of these timbers yielded dates of 1802 and 1805, closely coinciding with 1807 and 1808 documents that mentioned construction of a powder magazine, a granary, and a *sala de armas*, or arsenal. Beneath the lowest floor level of La Garita, archaeologists exposed the stone base of a *torreón* (defensive tower) that, on the basis of associated Pueblo pottery, they believe was built during the period of the Reconquest. The foundations of La Garita and the *torreón* had been dug into an earlier Indian pueblo on the hillside. Pottery associated with these ruins indicated a lengthy Pueblo occupation, ending in the Late Coalition or Early Classic period (ca. 1325–1350).

Along the Santa Fe River between Agua Fria and Cieneguilla are the remains of four of the ten Spanish and Mexican-period ranchos recorded by E. Boyd. The recent excavations at the Agua Fria School House site, mentioned above, produced pottery indicating a Spanish Colonial reoccupation of that area in the early to mid-eighteenth century. Other Colonial ranchos have been recorded in La Cienega. The artifacts recovered from rancho sites by Boyd, and from more recent tests at these sites performed under my direction and by David Snow, consist primarily of Pueblo-manufactured ceramics.

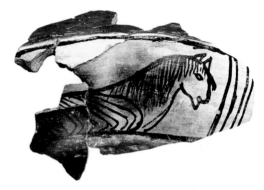

Fragment of a Pojoaque Polychrome *olla* showing unmistakable European influence. Excavated at a site near La Cieneguilla by E. Boyd and David Snow.

Tewa Polychrome soup bowl.

La Garita ruins, circa 1910.

To the lay person, archaeologists must seem to have an inexplainable fascination with potsherds. These Colonial sites are a good illustration of the importance of pottery. The ceramics from the Santa Fe River ranchos, as well as in the deposits dating to the Colonial occupation of the plaza, demonstrate the little-documented economic interdependence of Hispanic and Pueblo communities in seventeenth- and eighteenth-century Santa Fe. In the absence of an adequate supply of imports from Mexico, Hispanics turned to the Pueblos for many of their cooking pots and tablewares. In the Historic period, new Pueblo vessel forms such as the comal and rimmed soup bowl, new Pueblo design elements clearly derived from the Spaniards, and Mexican majolica patterns are found in the pottery recovered from Pueblo and Hispanic archaeological sites.

Ceramics continue to mark changes in trade practices in nineteenth-century archaeological deposits. The Santa Fe Trail, and later the railroad, brought new merchandise to the people of Santa Fe, introducing a wider variety of European ceramics, mass-produced glass, metal items, and other material goods. These changes are evident in the archaeological deposits of sites occupied after the opening of the Santa Fe Trail such as the foundations of the house underlying the Eldorado Hotel (formerly the Big Jo Hardware store) and some of the Santa Fe River ranchos investigated by this author. One of the most striking changes is the incorporation of American- and European-made ceramics into assemblages that, during the Spanish Colonial period, had consisted mainly of Pueblo-made ceramics. This change to mass-produced ceramic wares reflects a shift from the local exchange networks that had existed between and among Pueblo and Hispanic communities in Colonial times to the cash-based economy that began in New Mexico in the Mexican period and widened in the American period.

The Santa Fe Trail itself has been identified by archaeological surveys. Short segments of deeply rutted tracks found near the junction of the Old Las Vegas Highway and Old Pecos Trail are thought to be the remains of the trail.

Elsewhere in the city, archaeologists have recorded the remains of a brewery that flourished on Santa Fe's east side from about 1868 to 1896. They have also recorded the remains of acequias that served the farmsteads lining the Santa Fe River until not so long ago. Change is an inevitable part of the landscape, and archaeology is an essential tool for learning about the past and for preserving this knowledge for the future.

Visitors to Santa Fe are inspired by the multiethnic culture of the northern Rio Grande. Here the diversity of Native American, Hispanic, and Anglo-American cultures blends in distinctive regional foods, architectural styles, language, and life-styles. The archaeological resources of the northern Rio Grande are, like a fossil bed, a chronicle of the accommodations that these cultures have made between and among themselves. As we dig "down under" Santa Fe, we expand our understanding of the complex processes of cultural exchange and cultural change that have shaped this southwestern community over at least fourteen hundred years of human occupation.

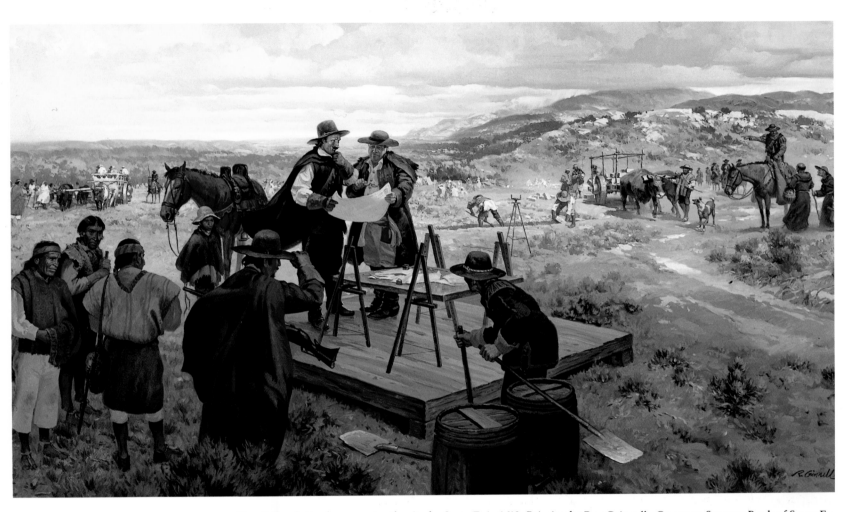

Don Pedro de Peralta surveying the site for Santa Fe in 1610. Painting by Roy Grinnell. Courtesy, Sunwest Bank of Santa Fe.

The Peralta-Ordóñez Affair and the Founding of Santa Fe

JOSEPH P. SÁNCHEZ

Between 1610 and 1615, in the newly founded villa of Santa Fe, a dramatic story evolved that would affect its history throughout most of the seventeenth century. The theme of this story, ecclesiastical resistance to civil control, originated with two powerful adversaries—Governor Pedro de Peralta, who founded La Villa Real de Santa Fe in 1610, and Friar Isidro Ordóñez. It was a conflict that would continue to plague the government of the province until 1680.

The founding of Santa Fe on the north bank of the Rio Santa Fe occurred twelve years after Spanish frontiersmen led by Juan de Oñate had settled La Provincia de Nuevo Mexico at San Juan de los Caballeros, on the upper Rio Grande. By 1600, the Spaniards had moved downstream to a new capital at San Gabriel, at the confluence of the Rio Chama and the Rio Grande. Sometime in the spring of 1610, Governor Peralta and several settlers from San Gabriel selected a site on the southern end of the Sangre de Cristo Mountains, and in accordance with the viceregal instructions of March 30, 1609, marked out "six *vecindades* [districts] for the villa and a square block for government buildings [*casas reales*, later known as the Palace of the Governors] and other public works."

After ordering that the villa be built on the new site, Peralta allowed the residents to elect four *regidores* (councilmen), two of whom were chosen as *alcaldes ordinarios* (judges) to hear civil and criminal cases within the boundary of the villa for "five leagues around." Of the two judges, one would serve

Santa Fe's "oldest house," on East De Vargas Street.

as *justicia mayor* (senior judge) of the villa. Accordingly, the incumbent councilmen would annually elect the *alcaldes* and councilmen who were to succeed them.

To ensure the development of the villa, Peralta empowered the *alcaldes* and councilmen for a period of thirty years to "apportion to each resident two lots for house and garden, two contiguous fields for vegetable gardens, two others for vineyards and olive groves, and in addition four *caballerías* [about 133 acres] of land; and for irrigation, the necessary water." In return for the grant, the settlers were obligated to establish residency for ten consecutive years without absenting themselves, under penalty of losing everything. Permission would be required from the *cabildo* (town council) for absences of more than four months, or one's grant could be assigned to someone else. Peralta, moreover, instructed the *cabildo* to elect an *alguacil* (sheriff) and a notary. Next, Peralta clarified the role of the *cabildo* regarding the creation of ordinances for the villa and the province. He told them that every conciliar action would be subject to his confirmation in conformity with the Laws of the Indies.

Much of the villa was built between 1610 and 1612. Later additions formed a large government-military compound containing arsenals, offices, a jail, a chapel, and the governor's residence and offices. The outer walls of adjoining structures, which also served as the defensive walls of the compound, enclosed two interior plazas whose dwellings were three and four stories high. Throughout its early history, the villa had only one gate, with a defensive trench in front of it. Despite its military character, Santa Fe was inhabited by farmers, artisans, traders, missionaries, and other frontiersmen and their Indian servants.

All roads in the province led to Santa Fe. The fortified town posted sentries in each of its four towers, two on the south wall and two on the north side of the quadrangle, who could watch the roads leading to the villa. They could see the Jemez Mountains to the west, and to the southwest, a singular peak known as La Tetilla. It marked La Bajada, the descent on the Camino Real de Tierra Adentro (Royal Road of the Interior), which began in Mexico City, crossed the central Mexican plateau, passed the pueblos of the lower Rio

Detail of a 1656 French map of New Mexico showing the Rio Grande flowing to the Pacific Ocean.

Copy of a portion of the viceregal
instructions of March 30, 1609.

Grande and La Cienega, and ended in Santa Fe. Other roads ran north from Santa Fe to Taos Pueblo, south to Galisteo, and southeast to Pecos.

Outside the enclosed plaza stood the homes of settlers, and on the southeast side, a Mexican Indian section called Barrio de Analco. *Analco* means "on the other side" in Nahuatl, referring to the other side of the Rio Santa Fe. Generally, Indian allies from Mexico who assisted missionaries or worked as servants to certain settlers resided there. Just south of Barrio de Analco were Las Milpas de San Miguel, the cultivated fields adjacent to the land of the chapel of San Miguel. The *milpas* were watered by the *acequia madre* (mother ditch), which was constructed to irrigate the fields south of the chapel of San Miguel. Before the Pueblo Revolt, Santa Fe's settlement does not appear to have extended southward beyond the *acequia madre*. On the north side of the villa, other fields had their attendant irrigation ditch.

The viceregal instructions of March 30, 1609, also advised Governor Peralta on the Indian policy for frontier New Mexico that had evolved since 1598. "No one shall have jurisdiction over the Indians except the governor or his lieutenant," wrote Viceroy Don Luis de Velasco. Regarding the *encomienda*, a grant to certain individuals to collect tribute from Indians, Peralta was permitted to make new grants if they did not interfere with those of the previous governor, Juan de Oñate. The orders to Peralta were explicit. Wrote Viceroy Velasco, "Inasmuch as it has been reported that the tribute levied on the natives is excessive, and that it is collected with much vexation and trouble to them, we charge the governor to take suitable measures in this matter, proceeding in such a way as to relieve and satisfy the royal conscience." The defense of Santa Fe and the province was the watchword of Peralta's Indian policy, as it would be for succeeding governors. "Under no circumstances," wrote the viceroy, "shall he give up the protection of the land and the colonists, but he shall try by peaceful means or by force to subdue the enemy or drive him out." Aside from military force, the pacification plan also enlisted the missionaries who already had been hard at work converting the Pueblo Indians to Christianity.

While Governor Peralta busied himself with establishing the villa, Friar Alonso de Peinado, Franciscan prelate of the New Mexico missions, supervised

Santo Domingo Pueblo.

the construction of a church for Santa Fe. Meanwhile, the settlers were content with a temporary church made of mud mortar and poles. In 1640 Friar Rosa Figueroa wrote that Peinado's church lasted a few years before it collapsed, whereupon the settlers had reverted to holding services in a makeshift church. There, noted Figueroa, the settlers and their servants gathered on Sundays and holy days of obligation in a wattled structure called a *xacalón* which also doubled as a *galerrón*, a granary. In 1627, under the watchful eye of Friar Alonso de Benavides, a new church called the *parroquia* was constructed.

Meantime, in 1610 Friar Peinado decided to establish the ecclesiastical headquarters for New Mexico at Santo Domingo Pueblo, south of Santa Fe. There, Franciscan prelates held their occasional chapter meetings and planned missionary activities throughout the seventeenth century. Once the civil and ecclesiastical capitals of the province had been established at Santa Fe and Santo Domingo, Governor Peralta and Prelate Peinado settled into an amicable administration of the province's temporal and spiritual needs. The halcyon days of 1610–1611, however, would not last long.

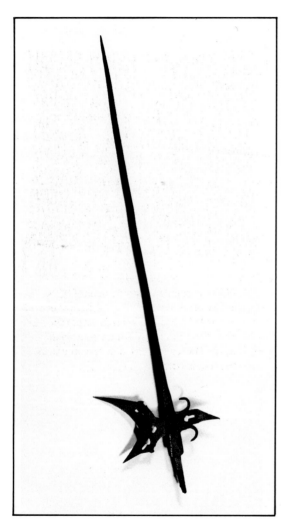

Spanish halberd.

Trouble between Church and State

Sometime in late summer of 1612, Friar Isidro Ordóñez arrived in Santo Domingo from Mexico City with twelve new missionary recruits. Before going to Santa Fe, he declared that he had orders to relieve Fray Peinado of his duties as prelate. Although the authenticity of Ordóñez's documents was questionable to Peinado, he accepted them as genuine. If they were not authentic, then the ambitious Ordóñez had deceived almost everyone in the province to gain control of the missions and force Governor Peralta to recognize him as the chief official of the province. Once at Santa Fe, Ordóñez presented Peralta with an order from the viceroy to direct his soldiers and settlers who so desired to leave New Mexico. To Peralta, the order was an incredible contradiction to his earlier instructions, which had authorized him to strengthen the area of Spanish occupation.

Everyone knew Friar Ordóñez's presence spelled trouble. When Governor Peralta heard Ordóñez had replaced Peinado, he was heard to exclaim, "Would to God the devil were coming instead of that friar!" The arrogant Ordóñez, who had served in New Mexico during the Oñate administration, was disliked by most of the friars as well. One of them, Friar Francisco Pérez Huerta, a notary, later examined Ordóñez's papers and declared them forgeries. The discovery of fraud came four years too late, however, for by that time Ordóñez had altered the character of the New Mexico province. His plan—to force the civil government out so that New Mexico would become exclusively a mission field—had almost succeeded.

The break between Friar Ordóñez and Governor Peralta occurred in May 1613, when the prelate interfered with the governor's privileged functions to collect the annual tribute of corn and blankets from the pueblos. As the tribute collectors bound for Taos went past Nambe Pueblo, north of Santa Fe, Ordóñez intercepted them, and under threat of excommunication, ordered them to return to the villa to hear mass, for the Feast of the Pentecost was at hand. Upon their return, Captain Pedro Ruiz, leader of the tribute collectors, reported to the governor, who ordered them back on the trail.

On Friday afternoon, May 24, 1613, Peralta and Ordóñez met in the plaza and publicly had words over the matter. Ordóñez had used the church calendar to countermand Peralta's authority, and the governor had responded by exercising his powers as captain-general to override his prelate's wishes. To strengthen his authority, Friar Ordóñez pulled out another surprise document from his robe. It named him as the agent of the Holy Office of the Inquisition for New Mexico. Angrily, he ordered the governor to bring back the tribute collectors under threat of excommunication. When Peralta refused, Ordóñez nailed a declaration of excommunication of the governor on the door of Santa Fe's church for all to read.

The settlers of the villa were in shock. They urged Peralta to seek absolution, but he refused. Friends and friars attempted to reconcile the two adversaries, but to no avail. One of the priests, Friar Luis Tirado, offered to absolve Peralta in the secrecy of the church so that he could be spared the humiliation of the ceremony before his peers, but he refused to do so on principle. Finally, under a truce the two men met, and in an abbreviated ceremony, Ordóñez absolved Peralta.

Before long trouble between the two men began anew. Everywhere Ordóñez looked, he found reason to criticize Peralta. Finally, Ordóñez met with Friar Tirado and hatched a plan to embarrass and discredit the governor in front of the citizenry of the villa. Closing the *convento* door, the two priests planned three Sunday masses, one of which was to be a main mass for captains and town officials. On Sunday Ordóñez and Tirado watched as the church filled with local dignitaries. Peralta's servants set the governor's chair on its platform in anticipation of his arrival. Suddenly, as the shocked congregation looked on, Friar Tirado stormed from the sacristy and ordered the chair thrown out of the church. When the governor arrived, he calmly ordered his chair placed immediately inside the rear of the church. While his political subordinates, nervous over the insult, sat toward the front of the church, friars Ordóñez and Tirado prayed the mass.

After Friar Tirado had read the gospel and was seated, Friar Ordóñez ascended the pulpit and delivered an impassioned homily against the governor,

Black wool embroidered manta (48″ × 54″) from Acoma Pueblo, made between about 1850 and 1860. Blankets of this nature were standard tribute items paid by the Pueblo Indians to the Spaniards in the seventeenth century.

much of it scandalous. Ordóñez claimed that his powers, granted through a papal concession, superseded those of the governor. He alone had the power to arrest, cast in chains, and punish anyone whom he considered an enemy of the church in New Mexico. "What I have told you," said Ordóñez, "I say for the benefit of a certain person who is listening to me who perhaps raises his eyebrows."

The congregation sat motionless. The ejection of the governor's chair, his presence at the rear of the church, and Ordóñez's stirring speech against Peralta's gubernatorial powers had made an indelible impression on those present. As soon as mass had finished, the villa was abuzz with new rumors of the friction between their governor and prelate.

That week a new confrontation occurred that permanently changed the political nature of colonial Santa Fe. The crisis reached a peak when Peralta heard that Ordóñez had called all his friars from the neighboring missions to the villa to arrest him for obstructing the business of the church. Previously, the two men had clashed over the collection of church tithes. One of Peralta's men-at-arms was also Ordóñez's syndic, a civilian representative of the church whose chief duty was to collect tithes. The governor ruled that the man's military duties came first, and, given the conflict of interest, the soldier could not fulfill his ecclesiastical obligations to collect the tithes. Ordóñez looked upon Peralta's decision as an offense against the church. A showdown was at hand, and Peralta decided to strike first.

Showdown at Morning Mass

On Tuesday morning, July 9, 1613, Peralta called upon loyal frontiersmen to grab their guns and meet at his quarters in the *casas reales*. When all had arrived, he explained that Ordóñez planned to arrest him and asked them to join him in ousting the friar from Santa Fe. After the meeting they followed him to the *convento* of the Santa Fe church.

Having watched the early morning commotion in the plaza from behind the *convento* walls, the priests warned their prelate. As Peralta's men walked across the plaza toward the *convento*, their wives, some of whom were crying

Petroglyph of early Franciscan, south of Santa Fe.

lest Ordóñez excommunicate their husbands, entered the church for morning mass. Meanwhile, Ordóñez had entered the sanctuary, stood at the altar, and turned his gaze on Doña Lucía, wife of Bartolomé Romero, a Peralta supporter. "Shut up," he told the weeping woman, as Friar Pérez Huerta later wrote, "words that today still ring in the church." Calmly, Ordóñez began the mass.

Outside, near the *portería* (*convento* gate), Friar Huerta watched as Peralta and his men came toward him. As the noisy frontiersmen approached, the friars retreated to the patio of the *convento*. Then the governor, wearing a coat of chain mail, armed with a sword in his belt, and carrying a pistolet (pocket pistol) in his hand, entered the *portería* with his men.

Having finished mass, Ordóñez, aware of the governor's purpose, grabbed a wooden cane and went out to face him. Immediately, Peralta ordered Ordóñez to return to his ecclesiastical headquarters at Santo Domingo Pueblo. The two men exchanged curses. Raising his pistolet, Peralta ordered his soldiers to enter the room and confiscate all weapons they could find. Ordóñez threatened to excommunicate them all, and Peralta countered with a threat to arrest the prelate. A scuffle ensued. Peralta grabbed Ordóñez's cape, and the friar slapped away his hand. Other priests moved in to defend their prelate. Friar Tirado took a sword from one of the soldiers and thrust it at Peralta, ripping his cape. While Ordóñez tried to hit the governor with his cane, Peralta raised his pistolet, but someone grabbed him by the wrist and the gun went off. The loud noise made by the discharging pistolet and the pungent smoke which filled the room brought everyone to a standstill. Friar Pedraza fell to the floor; he had been shot. Luckily, he had only been superficially wounded, but the shocking sight of a priest lying in pain on the floor cast a different character on the governor's actions. Slowly, Peralta's followers began to drift out of the room and away from him.

Outside, women were crying. The fight was over. That afternoon, before leaving for Santo Domingo, Ordóñez again posted a notice of excommunication for Governor Peralta and certain of his followers.

Friar Ordóñez called a meeting of all friars at Santo Domingo to determine their course of action. Four days later, he returned to Santa Fe hoping to persuade the settlers to arrest the governor on charges of attempted murder. He

Zia Pueblo, 1890.

was unsuccessful, for the settlers wanted no part of the scandalous behavior of their civil and ecclesiastical leaders. Ordóñez waited. He knew that sooner or later, Peralta would try to get a message out to Mexico City or go himself. The friars and their Indian friends watched the Camino Real from Santa Fe to see what the governor would do. Soon, some of the settlers joined Ordóñez at Santo Domingo, and a trap was set for Peralta.

The Fall of Peralta

A few weeks later, Peralta made his move and somehow got past Santo Domingo. Ordóñez vowed to track him down. Finally, at a camp near Isleta Pueblo, the friar and his self-appointed posse surrounded Peralta and his men and arrested them.

The governor and his men were taken to Sandia Pueblo and held as prisoners. Eventually, Peralta's men were released, but Peralta remained imprisoned until he escaped from his cell eight months later. Still shackled, Peralta crossed the rugged hill country east of Santo Domingo. After three days and two nights, he arrived in Santa Fe and took refuge at a friend's house. He was in poor health, for he had not eaten during the whole time of his escape, and he was so badly bruised by the shackle on one of his ankles that he could hardly walk. The freezing temperatures and snowfall of March 22, 1614, had further debilitated Peralta.

The next day, Palm Sunday, Ordóñez learned of Peralta's escape from Sandia. Immediately, he ordered a search of the villa. Peralta was found, dragged from his hideaway, put on a horse, and covered with a hide for his journey to Santo Domingo. There, Ordóñez assembled the Indians to show them that colonial justice applied to all. After making a public spectacle of Peralta, he returned the humiliated governor to his cell at Sandia Pueblo. He remained there until April 6, when he was transferred to a cell at Zia Pueblo.

Another year passed before news traveled up the Rio Grande that a new governor, Bernardino de Ceballos, had been appointed for New Mexico. Ceballos, a former admiral of the Spanish navy, arrived at Isleta, where he rested for two days before resuming his journey northward along the Camino Real. Before Ceballos reached Santo Domingo, a nervous Friar Ordóñez went out to meet him. Ceballos accorded the prelate small respect: "Are you the same *padre missionero* who represents himself as most powerful and exacting, whom I have met before?" The indignant Ceballos told him that he knew that his predecessor was held prisoner and that he would "release him and honor him . . . as a governor deserves." Ceballos was little impressed by Friar Ordóñez, but the prelate was not one to trifle with.

At Santo Domingo, Governor Ceballos was received by the pueblo amidst cheers and the ringing of church bells. Organ music poured out from inside the church as the Indian choir chanted prayers the friars had taught them. Ceballos entered the church and graciously listened to the choir. Shortly, the new governor was taken to his quarters in the *convento*, where he rested for two days before pushing on to Santa Fe.

Once at Santa Fe, Ceballos sent a letter to Peralta, still imprisoned at Zia, telling him that he regretted his absence and that he would bring him to the villa and honor him. Oddly, Peralta's release from Zia did not take place for another month, and then without the ceremonial reception Ceballos had promised him. Instead, within two weeks after his arrival, Ceballos began the *residencia*, the customary audit and review of Peralta's administration. Peralta's enemies did not miss the chance to testify against him. Ordóñez attended each session to intimidate pro-Peralta settlers into staying away from the proceedings, hoping that his presence would discourage any statements in favor of Peralta. His strategy worked, and all who testified were extremely careful of what they said concerning Peralta's relationship with Ordóñez. It was evident to Ceballos, however, that Ordóñez lacked inquisitorial authority and justification to arrest the former governor, or any governor for that matter.

The *residencia* continued into August. Each day of testimony worked against Peralta and his followers, who soon found that Governor Ceballos was not on their side. The historical record does not give a clue about Ceballos's change in allegiance other than to indicate that he demurred in his promise to honor Peralta. Perhaps Ceballos found more in common with the beguiling

Seal of the Mexican Inquisition.

Friar Ordóñez. In early November, Ceballos permitted Peralta to depart New Mexico—but not before friars Ordóñez and Tirado relieved him of some of his property.

Peralta was yet to suffer the final indignity. Once out of Santa Fe, past the pueblos of the Rio Abajo along the Camino Real, he took the route later called the Jornada del Muerto (journey of death). At a place called Agua del Perillo, a little northeast of El Paso, four soldiers sent by Ceballos and Ordóñez caught up with him and ransacked his cart for documents that might incriminate them. They found nothing. He had hidden his papers well. Sometime in the spring of 1615, Peralta arrived in Mexico City, and as soon as he could, reported to Spanish officials.

The Mexican Inquisition of 1615 pronounced against Ordóñez's pretensions, and on October 6, 1617, after two years of charges and countercharges, Friar Ordóñez was brought to Mexico City and reprimanded. Peralta was vindicated. But in many ways, Ordóñez had altered the course of New Mexico's history. From 1615 to 1680, Santa Fe continued to be the stage of troublesome and dramatic events, and almost every governor without exception suffered the test of ecclesiastical resistance to civil control.

Twelve Days in August

The Pueblo Revolt in Santa Fe

JOSEPH P. SÁNCHEZ

At dawn on August 10, 1680, curly-haired Pedro Hidalgo and Friar Juan Baptista Pio set out from La Villa de Santa Fe for mass at Tesuque Pueblo. They reached Tesuque at daylight and found it abandoned. Friar Pio decided to search for his congregation. Not far from the pueblo, he and his guard caught up with them near a ravine, which some of the Indians had already entered. Approaching them, Hidalgo noticed that the warriors were armed with lances, shields, bows, and arrows, and they were wearing war paint. Holding up a shield he had found along the way, Friar Pio walked toward them saying, "What is this . . . are you mad? Do not disturb yourselves; I will help you and die a thousand deaths for you."

The Spaniards tried to persuade them to return to the pueblo, but to no avail. The friar followed the Pueblos into the ravine, while Hidalgo, on horseback, rode over the ridge of it to intercept the Indians on the other side. Moments later, Hidalgo saw some warriors emerge from the mouth of the ravine. One of them, El Obi, carried the shield Friar Pio had taken into the ravine. Another warrior, Nicholas, painted with clay, had blood splattered on him. The Indians quickly grasped the reins of Hidalgo's horse and tried to pull him down, grabbing his sword and hat, but he managed to stay mounted. Spurring his horse down the hill, he broke away, dragging along those who clung to him. Arrows zipped past him as he made his escape. Riding hard, Hidalgo warned his fellow colonials on the farmlands leading to the villa that the Indians had taken up arms against the Spaniards. Hidalgo was the first to spread the alarm of the Pueblo Revolt.

Interpretation of the Pueblo Revolt by Parker Boyiddle.

Tesuque Pueblo.

The Pueblo Revolt of 1680 represented an accumulation of Indian resentments against a Spanish colonial occupation that had assumed total sovereignty over them. Long-standing grievances caused by an oppressive colonial economic system and Indian policy had worked to undermine the religious, political, and social traditions of the pueblos. Colonial-native relationships had not been exclusively antagonistic. In the eighty years since Juan de Oñate's founding of New Mexico, Spaniards and Indians had intermarried, and religious kinships such as *compadrazgo* (godparenting) had been established. Friendships and social associations had been formed among Spanish frontiersmen and their Indian counterparts. But such relationships were not enough to stifle Indian resentment against the injustices of colonialism.

Long-standing grievances were renewed by recent events, which were the immediate causes for the revolt. Soon after the Pueblo Revolt had begun, an Indian named Pedro García told Governor Antonio Otermín that the Tanos from Galisteo had planned to rebel "for more than twelve years . . . because they resented greatly that the friars and the Spaniards should deprive them of their idols, their dances, and their beliefs." At San Felipe Pueblo, other Indians told the governor that they had rebelled because of the ill treatment they had received from three Spaniards: Francisco Javier, Diego López Sambrano, and Luis Quintana. They complained that the three colonials often "beat them, took away what they had, and made them work without pay."

The colonials knew the history of such grievances and of several previous attempts by the Indians to liberate themselves from their Spanish lords. Red-haired Diego López Sambrano, a Santa Fean who was lucky to survive the rebellion with his wife and six children, said he had witnessed attempted revolts and punishments of Indian rebels "since the time of the government of don Fernando de Argüello (1644–1647), who hanged more than forty Indians." In 1650, a plot in which Pueblo Indians attempted to unite against the Spaniards had been discovered and quelled. Governor Hernando de Ugarte y la Concha had many Indians arrested from most of the pueblos in the province. After an investigation, nine leaders from Isleta, Alameda, San Felipe, Cochiti, and Jemez were found guilty and hanged. Others, recalled López, were "sold as slaves for ten years."

López remembered another rebellion on the Rio Abajo near Socorro during the administration of Governor Fernando de Villanueva (1665–1668), when the Piros "rebelled." One Piro named El Tanbulita had joined six Christian Indians and a band of Apaches in the "Sierra de Madalena," where they ambushed and killed six Spaniards. El Tanbulita and five others were captured and hanged, and several "others were sold and imprisoned," recalled López.

Soon after, one of the most serious of the rebellions was led by the Spanish-speaking Don Esteban Clemente, governor of the Tanos and Salinas pueblos, whom the "whole kingdom secretly obeyed." Clemente was extremely influential among Spaniards as well as Pueblos. He spoke several Indian tongues, and he was literate in Spanish. Organizing a "conspiracy which was general throughout the kingdom," said López, Clemente ordered the Christian Indians to drive all the Spanish horse herds in all of the jurisdictions to the sierras and leave the Spaniards afoot. The insurrection was to take place on the night of Holy Thursday. Then the Indians were to strike, reported López, "not leaving a single religious or Spaniard" alive. Clemente's plot was found out, and he was tried, convicted, and hanged while the Pueblos looked on helplessly. With Clemente gone, no one dared step forward to conspire against the Spaniards.

During the term of Governor Juan Francisco de Treviño (1675–1677), reported López, the Spaniards attempted to suppress Indian religious practices in New Mexico, claiming they "had continued their abuses and superstitions" long enough. López claimed that the natives "had bewitched the father preacher, Fray Andrés Durán," guardian of the *convento* of San Ildefonso, along with his brother and wife and an Indian interpreter named Francisco Guíter, "who had denounced the said sorcerers." Forty-seven Tewa Indians were arrested, four of whom admitted to the "witchcraft" worked against Friar Durán and his companions. The four, said López, were sentenced to death for the "above crimes and for other deaths which were proved against them." One was hanged at Nambe; another at San Felipe; a third *"hechicero"* (sorcerer)

Pueblo religious dance.

hanged himself while alone; and the fourth man was hanged at Jemez, remembered López.

The narrative of the 1675 "witch trial" did not end there. López explained how the execution and suicide of the four *hechiceros* and the detention of the remaining forty-three men had almost started a rebellion. Of the forty-three *hechiceros*, Governor Treviño ordered some released with a reprimand, and others "he condemned to lashings and imprisonment," recalled López. Among the prisoners was an angry headman known as Popé, who grew in resentment against the Spaniards.

Soon after the sentences were pronounced and the hangings had taken place, López recalled, "more than seventy Indians armed with *macanas* [clubs] and leather shields" entered the governor's office in the *casas reales* at Santa Fe. Filling two rooms, the warriors crowded together to hear the governor's response to their plea. As a sign of peace, the leaders presented him with an offering of "some eggs, chickens, tobacco, beans and some small deerskins." At first Governor Treviño refused the gifts, whereupon one of the Indians defiantly called out, "Leave them there if he does not want them." Wisely, the governor ordered Captain López to accept the gifts, and the natives got to the point of their visit. They asked the tough-minded colonial administrator to release the prisoners to them, requesting "that he should pardon them," and promising that "they would make amends." Treviño responded condescendingly: "Wait a while, children; I will give them to you and pardon them on condition that you foresake idolatry and iniquity." As a gesture of magnanimity, the governor gave them some woolen blankets and ordered the prisoners released to their pueblos. The Indians were satisfied and withdrew from his office.

A few days later, López saw some of the warriors who had pleaded for the prisoners' release. In a friendly way, López asked "why so many of your people came armed to see the governor." One of them replied, "We came determined to kill him if he did not give up the said prisoners, and on killing him, to kill the people of the Villa of Santa Fe as well." López learned that an ambuscade had been left in the nearby hills to support their escape. López asked where they would have gone, for the Apaches, who had intensified their raids against the pueblos and outlying Spanish farms, would have killed them in the sierras. The proud warriors gave him a chilling reply. "In order to defend the prisoners whom they asked for," wrote López, "they would have gone to the sierras even though the Apaches would kill them." That was how strongly they felt about colonial injustices.

Kiva, Taos Pueblo.

Rebellion

The lessons of past attacks, conspiracies, and rebellions were not lost on Popé. Fleeing harrassment from Captain Francisco Javier, a tribute collector, early in 1680 Popé hid in one of the kivas at Taos Pueblo. There, he communicated with spirits and formulated his plan to drive the Spaniards from New Mexico. Pedro Naranjo, a Keres Indian from San Felipe Pueblo, later recounted what he knew of the already legendary Popé. "It happened in a kiva at the pueblo of Los Taos," swore Naranjo. "There appeared to the said Popé three figures. . .called Caudi, another Tilini and the other Tleume." In awe, Naranjo described how Popé "saw these figures emit fire from all the extremities of their bodies." They told him to make a cord of maguey fiber "and tie some knots in it which would signify the number of days that they must wait for the rebellion." The cord was passed from one pueblo to the next, each of which accepted the righteousness of the revolt. After delivering the mandate to rebel, exclaimed Naranjo, the three spirits "returned to the state of their antiquity."

Convinced that secrecy was of utmost importance, Popé ordered the death of his brother-in-law, Juan Bua, because he had threatened to tell the Spaniards of the plot. Bua, from San Juan Pueblo, was not alone in his misgivings concerning the chances for a successful rebellion against the Spaniards. Some Pueblos thought Popé's plan was insane and refused to support it. Others warned their Spanish friends and relatives to prepare for a general uprising. When it finally occurred, some Indians helped Spaniards escape, and others fled with them.

The rebellion began with full fury on August 10, 1680. At a gallop, Pedro Hidalgo, with a cut on his neck from his escape near Tesuque Pueblo, pushed his jaded horse into the Santa Fe plaza and told of the death of Friar Pio at the hands of heavily armed Pueblo warriors. Angrily, Governor Otermín convened a council of war. The day before, having received warnings of a possible rebellion, he had started an investigation and devised a plan of attack should an uprising occur. Now it was too late, for he had not had time to call together his frontier men-at-arms who lived in the outlying farms, ranches, and haciendas near Santa Fe, who had also been caught off guard. The rebellion had begun, and the slaughter of Spanish women, children, friars, and other colonial frontiersmen had already taken on horrific proportions.

Those who could in the Rio Arriba region, between Cochiti and Taos pueblos, fled to the walled safety of Santa Fe. Luckily, Otermín had completed repairs on the villa's walls and gates eight days before the rebellion. Settlers in the Rio Abajo, between Cochiti and Socorro, were likewise caught unprepared. Many of them fled to the friendly pueblo of Isleta. On the eastern fringes of the Pueblo world toward the Great Plains, as on the western side of the province from Zia and Jemez across to Zuni and Oraibi, Spanish friars and settlers fell victim to the rebels.

Within four hours of Pedro Hidalgo's midday ride to warn Santa Fe of the rebellion, Governor Otermín acted to determine the extent of the revolt and protect the surviving settlers and their servants. He sent messengers to warn all settlers in the outlying districts to defend themselves. Meanwhile, he ordered the official of the armory in the villa to distribute "harquebuses, blunderbusses, swords, daggers, shields, and munitions" to all males who had none to defend the capital. Sentries were stationed on the rooftops and at the gates of Santa Fe and even in the church "for the protection and custody of the holy sacrament and the images, sacred vessels, and things pertaining to divine worship," wrote Captain Javier, secretary of government and war.

Detailed preparations were made for an Indian assault. In the next few days, particular attention was given the defense of the *casas reales*, presently known as the Palace of the Governors. Javier reported that the *casas reales* were "to be immediately intrenched, embrasures are to be made in the walls, watches set, and harquebusiers stationed on the roofs. The two small pieces of ordnance

Pueblo runners between Zia and Jemez, August 6, 1980, in the tricentennial celebration of the Pueblo Revolt.

will be placed in the doors of the *casas reales*, charged and mounted on their carriages, and aimed at the entrances of the streets."

Throughout the ordeal, Governor Otermín continued to receive accounts of harrowing episodes experienced by survivors who reached the villa. Among the first to report the rebellion were Nicolas Lucero and Antonio Gómez, who arrived in Santa Fe at five o'clock on the afternoon of August 10, 1680. They told the governor that they had been sent by the *alcalde mayor* of Taos to warn Santa Fe of the conspiracy. On the way there, they discovered that the *camino real* between Taos and the villa had been blocked by Pueblo warriors from Taos and Picuris—their first indication that a rebellion had begun. Forced to flee through the mountains, Lucero and Gómez reached La Cañada (Santa Cruz) and learned that the rebellion had spread to Santa Clara Pueblo, where two of eight men under Captain Francisco de Anaya had been killed as they were attending to a horse herd. Anaya and his men escaped, but herds of horses and cattle were driven off by mounted warriors from Santa Clara and Jemez pueblos. Lucero and Gómez also reported that the rebels had taken property from the fields and houses of Spaniards. Tight-lipped Otermín now knew that Taos, Picuris, La Cañada, Santa Clara, Tesuque, Jemez, and their vicinity were under attack.

Spanish coat of mail.

To learn the extent of "the damages and atrocious murders" which had taken place, wrote Javier, Governor Otermín ordered his high-ranking officer, Maestre de Campo Francisco Gómez Robledo, and a squadron of soldiers to La Cañada to investigate the rebellion at Tesuque, Cuyamungue, Pojoaque, and the rest of the pueblos on the road to Taos. As soon as they had collected their gear and supplies, they departed Santa Fe that evening.

Having reconnoitered the Indian pueblos and Spanish settlements on the road to Taos, Gómez Robledo and his men returned to Santa Fe on August 12 and confirmed the extent of the rebellion in the north. He reported that all of the pueblos from Tesuque to San Juan were in rebellion. A large number of warriors were fortified at Santa Clara, others were in the mountains near Tesuque, and the rest were scattered along the *caminos reales*, the various roads leading to the pueblos, to intercept Spaniards who fled on them. He reported

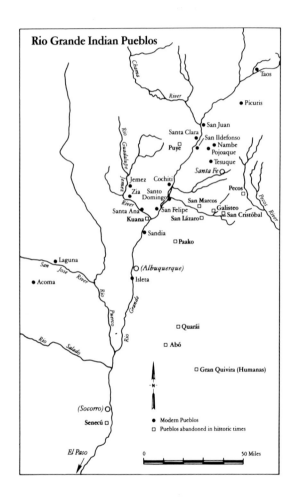

Rio Grande Indian Pueblos

Taos
Picuris
San Juan
Santa Clara
San Ildefonso
Puyé
Nambe
Pojoaque
Tesuque
Santa Fe
Jemez
Cochiti
Zia
Santo Domingo
Pecos
San Marcos
Galisteo
Santa Ana
San Felipe
San Cristóbal
Kuana
San Lázaro
Sandia
Paako
Laguna
(Albuquerque)
Isleta
Acoma
Quarái
Abó
Gran Quivira (Humanas)
(Socorro)
Senecú
El Paso

Chama River
Rio Grande
Rio Guadalupe
Jemez River
Pecos River
San Jose River
Rio Puerco
Rio Salado

• Modern Pueblos
□ Pueblos abandoned in historic times

0   50 Miles

that he had learned of the deaths of several friars and that many settlers had been killed at Pojoaque, Santa Clara, Nambe, and the outlying haciendas in the area. He also informed Otermín that many other Spaniards had been taken captive by the rebels.

Throughout the next few days, Otermín heard from the rest of his scouts whom he had sent out to assess the revolt in the Rio Arriba. From friendly Indians and captive rebels, the Spaniards learned that in a line south and west from Pecos to La Cienega by way of the Galisteo Basin, the Pueblos had rebelled and killed their Franciscan ministers as well as many settlers. Indeed, the picture looked grim for the settlers in Santa Fe, who now found themselves cut off from all routes of escape, for the rebels controlled all roads leading to the villa. The Spanish colonial capital seemed isolated and doomed.

From all the reports he had received, Otermín feared the imminent destruction of Santa Fe. He recommended that Friar Francisco Gómez de la Cadena, guardian of the church in the villa, consume the Holy Eucharist, take down the images and statuary, remove all sacred vessels and other religious paraphernalia for safekeeping in the *casas reales*, and close the church. Realizing the province had been lost, Otermín sent messengers through the rebel-held countryside to seek all survivors and bring them and whatever herds they could to the fortified villa.

Despite the onslaught, large numbers of Spaniards had been able to group together for common defense against the rebels and managed to stay alive. At Los Cerrillos, Sargento Mayor Bernabé Márquez and his men had been able to hold out, but they would not be able to do so for much longer. Otermín sent a small squadron to break the siege at Márquez's hacienda and escort the survivors to Santa Fe. Similarly, messengers reached Captain Luis Quintana and the besieged settlers at La Cañada, urging them to fight their way to the villa. Although the initial blow of the revolt had been devastating, through his scouts and messengers Otermín was able to account for various strongholds of Spanish settlers and summon them to the capital for their mutual protection.

Oddly, no word from the Rio Abajo had yet reached Otermín. Unknown to him, the three messengers he had sent to Lieutenant General Alonso García, in command of forces on the Rio Abajo, had all been killed. García and his settlers were under heavy attack between the pueblos of Alameda and Cochiti and were unable to get past the latter to assist Santa Fe. Deceived by the rebels that Santa Fe had fallen and that no one had survived, and realizing the extent of destruction in the Rio Abajo, García began to believe them. Likewise, Otermín thought that García and his settlers had been wiped out. The message to García was in the hands of the Pueblo warriors, who sensed victory. They had succeeded in splitting the Spanish command in New Mexico into two groups: one in Santa Fe, the other at Isleta.

The Siege of Santa Fe

Because the Pueblos first sought to control the countryside, the Spaniards had time to pull in survivors from their outlying strongholds. Two Christian Indians whom Otermín had sent with a message to García returned with the shattering news that the road to the Rio Abajo was held by the rebels, and five hundred Indians from Pecos, Galisteo, La Cienega, and other pueblos were on their way to attack Santa Fe. Shouting "God and Santa María are dead!" the rebel warriors had begun their march on Santa Fe with one aim: to kill the governor, the priests, and all the settlers.

The situation appeared even more ominous yet, when the Spaniards learned that the Apaches, motivated by revenge, had joined the pueblo rebels. Their grievances, although historical in nature, were sparked by a more recent event. Shortly before the general uprising, Captain Javier and a group of frontiersmen had seized a number of Apaches trading at Pecos Pueblo under a promise of safe conduct. Some were kept as slaves, and others were sent to Parral, in southern Chihuahua, to be sold in slavery. The Apaches were outraged, as were the Pecos, who feared reprisal from them and other Plains tribes. More importantly, the Pecos had depended on trade with the Apaches.

On the morning of August 13, Spanish sentries at Santa Fe spotted a host of rebel Indians in the fields of maize near San Miguel Church. Shortly, another group of warriors took Barrio de Analco and sacked the houses of Christian

De Vargas Street and San Miguel Church.

Mexican Indians. The besieged colonials recognized one of the Pueblo leaders, a man called Juan, a Tanoan from Galisteo. Wearing a sash of red taffeta from a missal and armed with a harquebus, a sword, a dagger, and a protective leather jacket, Juan approached the gates of Santa Fe on horseback to give Governor Otermín a message under a sign of truce. After some discussion, he was persuaded to enter the plaza to speak to the governor. Juan confirmed that all deaths and reports of destruction reported previously to the governor were true. He told him that the rebel army was on its way to offer the Spaniards the choice of one of two crosses, one red, the other white. The red cross meant continued war; the white cross, that the Spaniards would abandon the province.

Otermín responded that the Spaniards did not seek war and that the Indians could never cease to be Christians or forsake Spanish sovereignty. If they laid down their arms, Otermín said sternly, he would pardon the crimes they had committed. He admonished Juan and the rebels for what they had done, and he reiterated his demand that they disarm quietly. Nonplussed, Juan wheeled his horse around and left the plaza.

When Juan returned to Barrio de Analco, he told his warriors of the governor's response. Amidst sounding trumpets and shouts, they ridiculed the governor. Then, ringing the bells of the hermitage of San Miguel, they set fire to the small church and ransacked the houses near the walls of Santa Fe.

Meanwhile, Otermín, on the advice of his council of war, ordered an attack on the rebels before they could be reinforced by those whom Juan said were coming with the red and white crosses. As the Spanish soldiers left the gates, they were spotted by some other Indians, who swiftly fell upon them. Seeing that his men needed help, Otermín arrived with reinforcements to drive the Indians off. Then the Spaniards turned on the rebels who had set fire to San Miguel. They rushed the houses and killed many of the rebels in a fight that lasted most of the afternoon. Although many of the Spaniards were wounded, they were able to take back small herds of animals and some weapons to the villa.

Just as the Spaniards set fire to the houses so the rebels would not be able to use them, a large army of Taos and Picuris Indians attacked the villa from the other side, forcing Otermín to turn his attack against them. They were able to hold their positions, however. By dark the rebels had captured a number of houses behind the *casas reales* and set fire to the church, which Friar Gómez de la Cadena had abandoned earlier. Also, the Taos and Picuris bands had captured the cultivated fields and a few herds of cattle and sheep. The desperate colonials realized that part of their food supply had been lost to the enemy.

The siege of Santa Fe lasted nine days. Short of fodder and unable to spare water for their livestock, the colonials, who numbered about a thousand, let a number of their animals die. Worse still, the rebels cut off the water supply to the plaza and the *casas reales*. After two days without water, the colonials had to make a decision. Addressing the demoralized Spaniards in the plaza, Governor Otermín explained that their position was untenable and offered them their only alternative. Even if only a few of them should survive, they would have to fight their way out. It would be better to die fighting, he told them, than to die slowly of hunger and thirst, fearfully cooped up in the *casas reales* with the stench of the dead animals. Not only had the Spaniards lost control of the fields and water supply, but the rebels had actually captured a corner of the plaza and boldly lodged within the villa. By attacking at dawn, Otermín reasoned that they at least had a chance to escape.

The Battle of Santa Fe

At sunrise on August 20, 1680, the governor advanced with a small force of hand-picked veterans. Taken by surprise, the rebels were routed with great losses. By eleven o'clock, the siege had been broken. The Spaniards claimed to have slain three hundred rebels and put the rest of the Indian army to flight. Forty-seven rebels were captured, interrogated, and executed. The Spanish attack, bold as it appeared, was an act of desperation, for the rebels had numbered over 1,500 warriors.

After the battle, the Spaniards warily came out of the *casas reales*, leading the surviving livestock from the rooms where they had been kept for protection to the ruined fields to feed and water them. People and animals alike

The Acequia Madre, circa 1915. This irrigation ditch, which is still maintained, may date to Santa Fe's earliest decades.

had a chance to regain their strength. When the Spaniards saw their burnt homes, their ruined fields, and their desecrated church and hermitage, any hopes they may have had of remaining in Santa Fe were dashed.

Governor Otermín called a council of war to determine their course of action. Officers, soldiers, and priests filled the plaza. The priests, led by Friar Gómez de la Cadena, requested that Santa Fe be abandoned, for it would be impossible to hold it. Otermín's officers stated that the safety of the people, horses, and cattle could not be guaranteed if they remained in the gutted town. They had best leave before the rebels recovered from their setback.

On August 21, 1680, Otermín ordered that all clothing and livestock be divided among the defenders and their families and servants. Then an affidavit was signed to certify that Santa Fe had been abandoned after the council of war had collectively decided to rendezvous with Alonso García at Isleta. There, they

The front of the Palace of the Governors, circa 1920. Original construction of the palace dates to 1610.

would make a stand against the rebels. Marching in full military formation, more than one thousand men, women, and children departed Santa Fe. Otermín, who had been wounded twice, led his settlers southward on the Camino Real, which eighty-two years earlier had brought the Spaniards to New Mexico. Arriving at Isleta, they found the pueblo abandoned, for García had already retreated toward El Paso.

For more than a year, Otermín planned to reconquer the province. During the winter of 1681–1682, he led an expedition north to evaluate the destruction by the rebels. They reached Cochiti. In February 1682, suffering from his wounds and complaining of continuous headaches and eye problems, Otermín asked to be temporarily relieved to travel to Parral, Chihuahua, for treatment. His request was denied. In 1683 his gubernatorial term ended, and he rode out of El Paso as quietly as he had ridden into New Mexico.

Looking back on the Pueblo Revolt, colonial officials declared that the loss of New Mexico had tarnished Spanish pride. That pride had to be restored. Aside from the loss of the province, 21 clergymen and 380 settlers had been killed, and an undetermined number of colonists had been left behind as captives of the rebels. For the next twelve years, however, the Spaniards' principal accomplishment would be the establishment of El Paso.

The rebel Indians had also sustained significant losses during the revolt. Spanish accounts indicate that large numbers of warriors were killed and wounded. But for the Pueblos, the blow that had been delivered against a colonialism won by their subjugation and maintained by military superiority was worth the Pyrrhic victory. The fall of Santa Fe signaled the end of the first phase of Spanish colonial control of New Mexico. Twelve years later, after several attempts to regain the province, Governor Diego de Vargas led the army of the Reconquest from El Paso and once again took Santa Fe and New Mexico for Spain.

By Force of Arms

Vargas and the Spanish Restoration of Santa Fe

JOHN L. KESSELL

To Don Diego de Vargas, proud son of the illustrious house of Vargas of Madrid and twenty-year veteran of the royal service in the Indies, Santa Fe was a paradox. The mudbuilt capital of a poor kingdom—in Vargas's words, "last on earth and remote beyond compare"—Santa Fe had been lost to the rebellious Pueblo Indians for a dozen years, from 1680 to 1692. It offered him the promise of reconquest. And it became his prison. He loathed the place.

As reward for his heroic restoration of Santa Fe to the Spanish Crown in the early 1690s, Vargas expected promotion to Manila, Santiago de Guatemala, or Havana. But circumstances entrapped him. He aspired to improve his post, to escape what he termed the *zozobra*, the wrenching anguish, brought on by "the adversities and perils of that government of New Mexico." Yet, in 1704, when death overtook him, they buried Diego de Vargas in Santa Fe.

Today, we have more questions than answers about Santa Fe's physical appearance at the time of Vargas. What did the Indian pueblo superimposed on the former Spanish government buildings look like in 1692? What form had the villa taken by 1697, when Don Diego reluctantly surrendered authority to his successor? Where did the "parish church" stand in 1704? We do not even know at present the site of Diego de Vargas's grave.

A strutting aristocrat, the forty-seven-year-old Vargas acceded to the governorship of New Mexico in exile on February 22, 1691, at miserable, unkempt El Paso. He proved decisive, fearless, and vain. Described twenty years earlier, on the eve of his departure from Madrid, as a young nobleman of aver-

Don Diego de Vargas Zapata y Luján Ponce de León.

Spanish petroglyph at El Morro, New Mexico. "Gen. Don Diego de Vargas was here, who conquered all New Mexico for our Holy Faith and the Royal Crown, at his own expense, in the year 1692."

age stature, straight hair, and broad face, Don Diego had a distinguishing feature. He could not pronounce certain words correctly. He lisped.

Appointed to the New Mexico post for his outstanding record in two mining districts of New Spain and an appropriate payment to the Crown, Vargas enjoyed the full confidence of the viceroy in Mexico City, the Conde de Galve, a personal acquaintance. Galve's grand design to expand and defend the borderlands of New Spain encompassed the explorations of Jesuit Father Eusebio Francisco Kino on the Sonora-Arizona frontier, west of New Mexico, and the occupation of east Texas and the Gulf Coast to thwart French colonization of Louisiana. Restoration of New Mexico, as a buffer to safeguard the silver mines of northern New Spain, was crucial to the plan.

The lightning first round in 1680 of the Pueblo-Spanish War, which saw the Spaniards driven from the colony to wretched exile in the El Paso district, had not been avenged. During the second round, an ill-advised attempt at reconquest in 1681 failed ingloriously. More recently, two of Vargas's predecessors had led forays up the Rio Grande, resulting in bloody Spanish victories at the pueblos of Santa Ana in 1688 and Zia in 1689.

The next round of the Pueblo-Spanish War was up to Vargas. The new governor planned a two-stage reconquest: first, a military reconnaissance to repossess the pueblos, by force of arms if necessary, and then a larger colonizing expedition to reoccupy Santa Fe and the former kingdom of New Mexico.

Frustrated for a year and a half by problems of supply, recruiting, Apache warfare to the west, repair of the diversion dam at El Paso, and a hundred other details, Don Diego delayed publicly proclaiming the first expedition until the feast day of St. Lawrence—August 10, 1692, the twelfth anniversary of the Pueblo Revolt. Then, he moved with dispatch.

Ritual Repossession, September 13, 1692

In the early morning darkness of Saturday, September 13, Vargas cautiously led a slender column of forty mounted soldiers, ten armed citizens, fifty Indian auxiliaries, and two blue-robed Franciscan friars through the fields adjoining the plaza of the former Spanish capital. No one was to open fire, on pain of death, unless Don Diego unsheathed his sword.

North of the plaza loomed the massive pueblo and stronghold that the Indian occupants—mostly Tanos from the Galisteo Basin and some Tewas—had built over the top of the rambling old governor's "palace" and *casas reales.* The Spaniards' cry in unison, "Glory to the Blessed Sacrament of the Altar!" sent the Indians inside scurrying to the parapets.

With the aid of Spaniards who knew the native language, Vargas called out that he had come in peace to pardon them and accept their renewed obedience to God and king. The defenders could just make out the cross and the banner of the Blessed Virgin as the first thin light of morning shone over the mountains to the east. They were defiant. At the sound of the Spaniards' trumpet and drum, they began shouting obscenities.

Vargas, dividing his small force to surround the stronghold, stationed himself before the main gate and tried to negotiate. Armed natives from other pueblos gathered on the hills nearby. The grimly determined Spaniard now ordered the ditch supplying water to the stronghold cut and a small cannon and a mortar brought up.

A less decisive commander might have withdrawn. Vargas relied instead on extraordinary boldness and personal diplomacy to exploit the Indians' disunity. Narrowly averting battle, he won the day. As the native leaders came out to make peace, Don Diego dismounted to embrace them. The anxious confrontation had lasted from four in the morning until late that afternoon.

Next day, in the first of two enclosed patios of the high, multistoried stronghold at Santa Fe—and later in most of the other pueblos of the kingdom—Diego de Vargas, resplendent in European court dress, proclaimed the ceremonial repossession before hundreds of wary Pueblo Indians. The Franciscans then absolved the Indians of their apostasy, celebrated the Mass, and baptized the dozens of children born since 1680. Vargas stood as godfather to daughters and sons of Pueblo leaders, thereby, in Roman Catholic terms, binding the latter to him as *compadres.*

Remnants of a rosary found in the graveyard of the church (circa 1700) at Pecos National Monument.

Statue of Nuestra Señora del Rosario,
known as La Conquistadora.

Halfway through his symbolic reconquest, an exultant Don Diego wrote to the viceroy from Santa Fe, enclosing a copy of his campaign journal to date, a chronicle of hardship and heroics. The same day, October 16, he penned a letter to his son-in-law in Madrid, Don Ignacio López de Zárate, a well-placed royal bureaucrat. He wanted to make certain the king learned promptly of "such a triumph and glory." Surely his majesty would wish to reward him appropriately. "I therefore give him the news of this conquest, of the pueblos and districts I have restored to his royal crown, and the number of people baptized."

Conveyed by fast courier to Mexico City, the news set off a grand celebration. The celebrators, including the Conde de Galve, seemed not to care that this was no more than a ceremonial reconquest. By Christmas of 1692, Diego de Vargas and his weary force would be back in El Paso, but at the time no one could foresee the desperate clashes to come.

Even today, despite our historical vantage, we tend to forget what happened next. By commemorating only the "bloodless" reconquest in the annual Santa Fe fiesta, we do neither the Pueblo Indians nor Vargas and the colonists the honor they deserve. By ignoring the bloody sequels to 1692 and the end of the Pueblo-Spanish War, we distort the past and disregard the sacrifices demanded of others to achieve the plural culture we cherish so much.

There is no reason to believe that the Pueblo leaders duped Don Diego in 1692 or that he failed to recognize the difference between ritual repossession and actual occupation. With characteristic zeal, he threw himself into the recruitment and supply of a colonizing expedition, generously supported by Galve and the royal treasury, and, with characteristic impatience and overconfidence, he led it north in 1693 too late in the year.

But Vargas knew that the Pueblo Indians were capable of repeating their violent acts of 1680. He had advised the viceroy in 1692 that to reoccupy the kingdom with fewer than five hundred families and a hundred soldiers would be "like casting a grain of salt into the sea." Still, in the motley caravan that forded the river at El Paso and crawled north in October of 1693, there were only seventy families. None would forget the suffering of that journey.

Wagons broke down, provisions ran so low that the people were reduced to trading their belongings to Indians for food; rumors of ambush abounded; and, worst of all, winter came early with freezing wind, snow, and deadly, cold silence. In contrast, smoke from a hundred fires rose above the secure Pueblo Indian stronghold in Santa Fe, at the base of towering, gray-blue mountains.

Ordering colonists, soldiers, and friars to make camp on the frozen field where Rosario Chapel stands today, Vargas tolerated two agonizing weeks of negotiations. Nuestra Señora del Rosario, the small statue still venerated as La Conquistadora, waited in a wagon to be restored to her throne in Santa Fe. Meanwhile, malnutrition and exposure took a ghastly toll. Infants died and were buried under the snow. Bitter resentment gripped the Spanish camp. The Pueblo Indian occupants of Santa Fe, it was obvious, had no intention of vacating their homes.

The Battle of Santa Fe, December 29, 1693

The fiercely fought battle for Santa Fe broke out on the morning of December 29, 1693. Had the Pueblo Indians of New Mexico united against Vargas, as they had in 1680, the outcome would have been different. Instead, motivated by their traditional enmities and the advantages of honors, protection, and trade offered by the returning Spaniards, they split. One hundred and forty fighting men from Pecos Pueblo, enemies of the occupants of Santa Fe, arrived just in time to join the Spanish assault. Taking the parapet above the main entrance, the attackers burned the heavy wooden gate and rushed into the first patio, overrunning the round, partially subterranean kiva. The previous year, at Vargas's orders, this kiva had been whitewashed for use as a temporary chapel, but the friars, objecting to the heathen rites that had taken place within, had refused to consecrate it.

That afternoon, having secured one entire houseblock and the front patio, the attackers repulsed outside two assaults by Indian allies of the defenders, probably Tewas. Inside, they constructed ladders. Night interrupted the fighting. Before dawn on December 30, Spaniards scaled and won all the

Statue of Spanish conquistador in full armor.

rooms facing on the first patio. From the rooftops of the houseblock separating the two patios, they could look down into the second one, where the defenders had fortified another kiva. It, too, was overrun. In a room nearby, José, the wounded native governor of Santa Fe, garroted himself. By mid-morning the battle was over. Vargas ordered a cross erected above the main entrance and the royal banner flown from the walls. The Spaniards had won back their capital.

It took twenty soldiers and thirty Indians the rest of the day to inspect and inventory all the rooms of the four houseblocks. More than a thousand people, they estimated, could be housed within. The maize, beans, and other provisions they discovered were carried to a kiva that had been swept out to serve as the temporary public granary. Vargas ordered seventy of the defenders, who had refused to surrender, taken out behind the stronghold and executed. Some four hundred others, who had given themselves up, he distributed among the soldiers and colonists for ten years of servitude. Although soldiers would set out in the future from Santa Fe to fight under the banners of successive sovereigns—Spain, Mexico, and the United States—never again after its restoration was the capital of New Mexico the scene of a major battle.

Vargas Imprisoned

In the flush of victory, Vargas could not have imagined how his fate would change. On September 30, 1698, evidently somewhere in the remodeled complex known as the governor's palace, confined to quarters and desolate, Don Diego found two blank pages in a book and wrote a desperate letter to his son-in-law in Madrid. He had been held prisoner for eighteen months, a fate he compared figuratively to captivity in Algiers, where Spain's traditional enemies in the Mediterranean, the Turks, often cast Spaniards into prison. His clothing, his slaves, and his mules had been sold at auction. Even the Franciscan friars were prevented from visiting him. He felt utterly forsaken. His particular patron, the Conde de Galve, had retired as viceroy more than two years earlier and died in Spain. Vargas himself, considering his periodic bouts of typhus and other maladies, feared that he might not live much longer.

Historic-period leg irons.

"May God keep Your Lordship and my daughter, Isabel, and the grand-children, to whom I give my blessing," he wrote, "for I do not know if I shall see them again." Because his jailers had taken even paper from him, this one letter would have to suffice for all the relatives. "I made my will in Madrid in 1672," he reminded his son-in-law. If God should take him, he wanted his wishes carried out. The reconqueror of New Mexico had lost all hope.

In large part, Vargas had himself to blame for his imprisonment. Early in July of 1697—more than sixteen months after his five-year term of office as governor of New Mexico had expired—Don Diego, so convinced that the Crown had rewarded him, at the very least, with an extension in office, had turned over authority to his successor grudgingly.

Of relatively humble origin, the forty-year-old Don Pedro Rodríguez Cubero had worked his way up through the ranks. His royal appointment to succeed Don Diego, which had been challenged in Mexico City by Vargas's lawyer and delayed, was completely in order. Furthermore, he was empowered to conduct the mandatory judicial review of his predecessor's administration. After that, he heard criminal charges against Vargas, purportedly brought by the six-member Santa Fe municipal council. Misuse of royal funds, abuse of authority, favoritism, fomenting sedition among colonists and Indians—the accusations were serious. On October 2, 1697, Don Pedro jailed Don Diego.

Whether or not Rodríguez Cubero coerced the council members and others to testify against their former governor, as Vargas charged, not a few of the colonists hated the haughty, unbending Don Diego. He had held the power of life or death over them for six years. He should never have led them upriver from El Paso so late in 1693. And three years later, he should have listened to the friars and anticipated the second rebellion of the northern pueblos. On both occasions, his arrogance had cost the lives of their relatives. For his part, Don Diego considered the council members "of very low class and menial offices—tailors, a shoemaker, and a lackey—poor and base people." New Mexicans, he assured his son-in-law, were "people of very bad qualities and worse behavior . . . given to swear falsely, perjuring themselves in exchange for a young goat."

Jemez Pueblo, 1847.

In Spain, meanwhile, Vargas's notable accomplishments were being discussed in the king's councils. After the brutal battle and executions at Santa Fe—which the Conde de Galve, upon review, had judged unavoidable—Vargas, using Santa Fe as a base of operations, had carried his reconquest, the final stage of the Pueblo-Spanish War, to Indians fortified on steep-sided mesas. Aided by the Pecos and other Pueblo auxiliaries, he had won two pivotal victories on or about July 25, feast day of St. James, Spain's patron saint—first against the Jemez Indians in 1694 and then against the Tewas near Santa Clara in 1696. He had vowed to make a pilgrimage to the saint's shrine at Santiago de Compostela whenever he returned to Spain. Following in the footsteps of his father and most of the males in his family, Don Diego sought knighthood in the military Order of Santiago. But he failed, evidently because of the opposition of an influential member, a first cousin of Pedro Rodríguez Cubero.

Vargas had ridden out from Santa Fe to reinstall Franciscan missionaries at as many as fifteen of the pueblos and to personally encourage the Indians to rebuild their mission churches. He had welcomed two delayed contingents of colonists. The first, 60 families, some 225 people, were recruited in Mexico City and reached Santa Fe on June 23, 1694. These the governor led north the following spring to found the colony's second chartered municipality, Santa Cruz de la Cañada, near present-day Española. Forty-four more families brought up from Sombrerete, Zacatecas, and other mining towns by Juan Páez Hurtado, Vargas's trusted lieutenant, finally entered the capital on May 9, 1695.

The winter of 1695–96 was a time of suffering. Food shortages, an epidemic of "plague," and rumors that the northern pueblos were plotting war again kept the colonists on edge. By this time, between 1,500 and 2,000 men, women, children, and Indian servants were concentrated in and around Santa Fe; Santa Cruz de la Cañada, twenty-five miles to the north; and Bernalillo, forty miles down the Rio Grande. Outnumbered by the Pueblo Indians ten to one, many of the colonists were thoroughly disillusioned by the hardships of New Mexico and wanted to desert. That December, Vargas summoned Santa Fe officials to his sickbed in the governor's palace and dictated a will. But his time had not yet come, and he recovered.

Early in June 1696, the Franciscans' dire predictions came true. The Pueblo Indians of the north rose again with all the fury of 1680, killing five missionaries and twenty-one civilians. Don Diego and his soldier-colonists, aided by men from five allied pueblos, fought back fiercely. By November, the fighting had ended. Pueblo Indian resistance was broken. Authorities in Mexico City, jolted by the prospect of losing New Mexico again, now committed further aid to the beleaguered colony. By 1697, the Reconquest had at last been achieved, and the Pueblo-Spanish War, which had erupted so furiously in 1680, was finally over.

While he languished in captivity in Santa Fe, Don Diego was belatedly honored in Spain. In 1698, the king granted him a noble title of Castile, Marqués de la Nava de Barcinas, a name Vargas took from two of his family's rural properties near Granada. Recipient as well of a considerable annuity, he failed to win promotion in the royal service. Instead, he was reappointed to succeed Rodríguez Cubero as governor of New Mexico. Not until the summer of 1700, after he had been held in leg irons for five months, did Vargas secure his release. The reconqueror, after "three lost years," wiped the dust of Santa Fe from his boots. Reanimated, he rode south not to a hero's welcome, but to answer in Mexico City the charges against him.

Three leagues north of the viceregal capital, the former governor experienced an emotional reunion. He was met by a dashing, twenty-nine-year-old Spanish cavalry officer, formerly a noble page to two queens of Spain. Don Diego had last seen the captain as a twenty-month-old infant. His only surviving legitimate son and heir had grown up in his absence. Don Juan Manuel had journeyed to New Spain to get to know his father and to convince him to come home. The elder Vargas, wrote Juan Manuel admiringly, looked "so fit that those who had known him were amazed, for the hardships he has undergone were enough to have put him in his grave." Now, beholding his son, Diego de Vargas could not speak.

For three years, Vargas resided again in Mexico City, accepting the generosity of wealthy friends and pursuing his exoneration. He already had a residence there. Since the late 1670s, he had provided a home in the capital for a woman companion. His wife in Spain, Doña Beatriz Pimentel de Prado, had died in 1674, the year after he had sailed. Even though he was a widower, he had chosen not to marry the woman in Mexico City, who may have been Nicolasa Rincón, even though he had three children with her. He would never give up the hope, he later admitted, of returning honorably to Spain and again marrying someone of his temperament and social station.

Securing passage home for Don Juan Manuel in 1702, Vargas went further in debt to outfit the captain "as if he were the son of a grandee of Spain." He indulged his son. When Juan Manuel's lover died in childbirth, Don Diego paid the funeral expenses and took care of the baby, who, he confessed, was "the very image" of him. Then, tragic news arrived from Havana. Vargas's beloved son had contracted a respiratory illness aboard ship and died. Utterly disconsolate, for a brief time Don Diego contemplated suicide. Then, drawing on his deep sense of honor and family responsibility, he pulled himself together to face the charges against him in court.

Vargas Exonerated

With the advent late in 1702 of a new viceroy, the Duque de Alburquerque, who knew Vargas's daughter and son-in-law and who personally attended the hearings, the proceedings moved more swiftly. The verdict, read in the spring of 1703, elated Don Diego. He was fully exonerated; he owed nothing to the royal treasury; in fact, a considerable balance remained in his favor. The authorities had dropped all charges against him and assessed Rodríguez Cubero and the villa of Santa Fe court costs.

Free at last to put his reappointment into effect, Vargas swore that, despite the injustices he had suffered, he would not govern vindictively. That summer, accompanied by his two natural sons, Don Diego rode north again for Santa Fe, where, at the age of sixty, he took office a second time on November 10, 1703.

To hear Vargas tell it, Rodríguez Cubero had all but ruined the colony. He had let Vargas's defensive works in Santa Fe fall into disrepair. He had allowed the presidial garrison to disperse, implying that the men had previously lived

Don Francisco Fernández de la Cueva Enríquez, duke of Alburquerque and viceroy of New Spain, 1702–1711.

in barracks. The church was in abhorrent condition. Leaving New Mexico by a westerly route to avoid meeting his antagonist on the road, Don Pedro hastened to Mexico City to prepare for his next assignment. But he died there in 1704. Meanwhile, the humble people of New Mexico welcomed the restored Don Diego, first Marqués de la Nava de Barcinas, in his words, "with applause and general acclamation."

Two months after his reinstatement in Santa Fe, Diego de Vargas had a premonition of death. In mid-January, he wrote a series of letters to family members in Spain, putting his affairs in order. "After all," he mused, "we are mortal." By mid-April, he was dead. He had gone on campaign. Pursuing Apaches in the bosque some forty miles south of Bernalillo, "he suffered," according to Juan Páez Hurtado, "a severe attack of fever caused by stomach chills." It may have been dysentery. Carried back to Bernalillo, he hung on for four days. Then, on April 8, 1704, at about five in the afternoon, Vargas expired.

In his final will, he had asked to be buried in the church of Santa Fe "in the main chapel beneath the platform where the priest stands." Unfortunately, the site of the church in 1704 is unknown. It may be that Vargas's bones were transferred ceremonially to the new parish church in use a dozen years later in the vicinity of the nineteenth-century cathedral. Wherever the reconqueror's remains came to rest, it is unlikely, given successive reconstructions, that they lie undisturbed.

In many ways, New Mexico was different in the years after Vargas from what it had been before. Out of the tumult and shifting for survival, a gradual if sometimes fitful change in human relations had begun to take place—from crusading intolerance to pragmatic accommodation. The names of native peoples and colonists who found themselves forced to coexist in the 1690s and in succeeding generations are still present in New Mexico three centuries later.

By restoring Santa Fe, seat and symbol of government authority since 1610, Don Diego de Vargas reestablished Spain's presence in the kingdom of New Mexico. No matter that he never liked the place. Here, at least, his memory lives on.

Coat of arms of General Vargas.

De Yndio y Mestiza
Coyote.

Españoles, Castas, y Labradores

Santa Fe Society in the Eighteenth Century

ADRIAN H. BUSTAMANTE

Friar Francisco Atanacio Domínguez, recently appointed father visitor of New Mexico, and his small retinue passed through Quemado (now Agua Fria) on a windy day in March 1776. There he was told that they were only one league from the villa of Santa Fe. Friar Domínguez, who had been raised in Mexico City, expected Santa Fe to have the conveniences that other capitals of the viceroyalty of New Spain afforded. But as the travelers continued, they saw only oxen, horses, and burros grazing on dried corn stalks and wheat stubble, and at the edge of the fields, adobe houses where the owners of these small ranches lived. Even when they reached the villa itself, they found little to distinguish Santa Fe from the other rural settlements they had passed since leaving north central Mexico. Fields lined the river and even surrounded the main plaza. This, the seat of government for Spain's northernmost province in the Americas, was to him nothing but a village practicing subsistence agriculture.

In his official description (published in 1956 in *The Missions of New Mexico, 1776*) Friar Domínguez noted,

> This villa . . . in the final analysis . . . lacks everything. Its appearance is mournful because not only are the houses of earth, but they are not adorned by any artifice of brush or construction. To conclude, the Villa of Santa Fe (for the most part) consists of many small ranches at various distances from one another, with no plan as to their location, for each owner built as he was able, wished to, or found convenient, now for the little farms they have there, now for the small herds of cattle which they keep in corrals of stakes, or else for other reasons.

Opposite page: Eighteenth-century Spanish illustration of New World *castas,* or racial mixtures. Depicted here, an Indian man with his "mestiza" wife and their "coyote" child.

This 1865 photograph of East San Francisco Street gives a sense of how Santa Fe may have appeared a century earlier. *Opposite page,* map of Santa Fe by José de Urrutia, 1766.

In spite of what has been said, there is a semblance of a street in this villa. It begins on the left facing north shortly after one leaves the west gate of the cemetery of the parish church and extends down about 400 or 500 varas. Indeed, I point out that this quasi-street not only lacks orderly rows, or blocks, of houses, but at its very beginning, which faces north, it forms one side of a little plaza in front of our church. The other three sides are three houses of settlers with alleys between them. The entrance to the main plaza is down through these.

Friar Francisco's observations on the layout of the village are confirmed by a map of Santa Fe drawn by Joseph de Urrutia in 1768. It was totally unlike farming communities in Europe and Mexico, which consisted of rows of houses surrounding a central plaza. Many medieval European villages had been walled for protection, and in the seventeenth century, Santa Fe too had been a walled town. But by the eighteenth century, the defensive wall was gone, and the people spread out to pursue their livelihood. Up and down both sides of the Santa Fe River, they built homes near their fields to keep marauding bears, raccoons, porcupines, and other wildlife from laying waste to the crops. They also had to guard themselves against their fellow citizens; in some cases, the governor sentenced those caught stealing their neighbors' produce to be pilloried on the plaza, with the stolen fruits and vegetables hung around their neck.

This decentralized settlement pattern caused many problems for the governors of New Mexico, who wanted to fortify Santa Fe against attacks by hostile Indians. In 1768, when Comanches persistently threatened the colony, Governor Pedro Fermín de Mendinueta ordered Santa Fe's residents to move closer to the plaza. Possibly because no Indians had attacked the villa since the Pueblo Revolt of 1680, the populace refused, staying close to fields and livestock in their *ranchitos.*

When Mexico City officials sent Don Juan Baptista de Anza to Santa Fe to deal with the Indian problem in 1777, the new governor initiated what historian Marc Simmons has called "the first attempt at urban renewal in Santa Fe." Anza wanted to move the plaza, the *casas reales* (Palace of the Govenors),

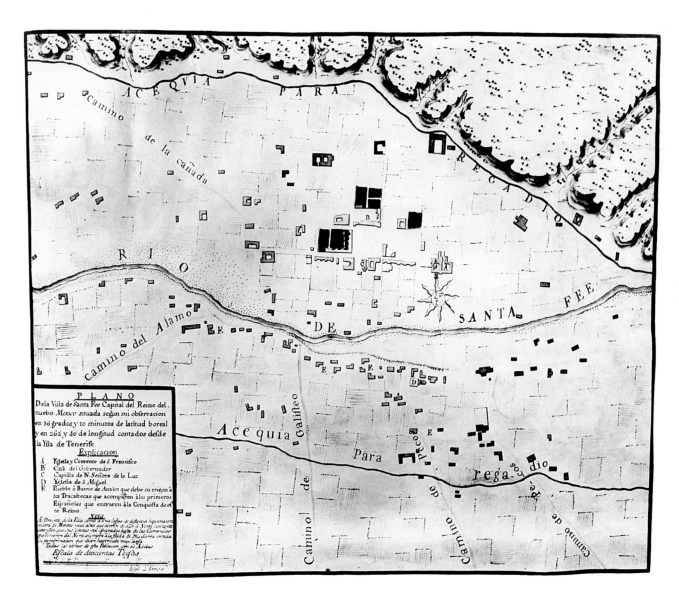

PLANO
Dela Villa de Santa Fee Capital del Reino del.
nuebo Mexico situada segun mi observacion
en 36 grados y 10 minutos de latitud boreal
y en 262 y 40 de longitud contados desde
la Ysla de Tenerife.

Explicacion

A. Yglesia y Convente de S. Francisco
B. Casa del Gobernador
C. Capilla de N. Señora de la Luz
D. Yglesia de S. Miguel
E. Pueblo ò Barrio de Analco que debe su origen à
los Tracaltecas que acompañaron à los primeros
Españoles que entraron à la Conquista de es-
te Reino.

Nota

Escala de docientas Toesas

and all other public buildings across the river to Barrio de Analco, which surrounded San Miguel Church, and which shows clearly on Urrutia's map. Anza felt that the higher ground south of the river was easier to defend than the area around the plaza. Again, the citizens refused to move. Anza abandoned the project, and the locals continued to build their homes where it was convenient for their livelihood.

Santa Fe Society, 1790

The 1790 census of New Mexico, the most complete of the period, shows that farming was the most common occupation in Santa Fe, which had a population of 2,542. Out of 564 heads of family, 262 (46 percent) were listed as full-time farmers (*labradores*). Day laborers, accounting for another 60 heads of household, also contributed to the farming economy.

For some reason, the census did not give the occupations of many of the heads of household, but those mentioned—adobemakers, carpenters, blacksmiths, barrelmakers, lumbermen, muleskinners, shoemakers, weavers, and tailors, to name a few—demonstrate the self-sufficiency of the villa. Interestingly, the census names two hunters, but no butchers. Families probably did their own butchering, as they do to this day in the villages of northern New Mexico, although not to as great an extent.

The census lists only one schoolteacher, who was probably hired as a tutor by the few families who could afford to pay for his services. As farmers, most Santa Feans saw little value in formal education. Boys were expected to learn farming or some other practical trade, and girls learned how to take care of the household. The few families who did send their children to Mexico to be formally educated were very much in the minority. Literacy was the exception. If someone needed a document written, they went to a scribe, who worked for a fee. The lack of educational facilities would always be endemic to colonial Santa Fe. As far as the needs of the society were concerned, a good farmer or herdsman was worth ten scribes.

Typical *carreta*, or cart, formerly used by New Mexico farmers.

Until relatively recent times, sheep and goats were commonly used to thresh wheat.

It is not surprising that the census also lists only one full-time merchant. In 1790, New Mexico suffered from an imbalance of trade with Mexico. The merchants of Chihuahua and other parts of the Mexican interior charged more for their goods than Santa Feans could for theirs. However, local trading had always been important in New Mexico in late fall and winter, after the crops were in. At well-attended trade fairs in Pecos and Taos, people bartered for goods, and very little money circulated. For example, a bridle could be had for two buffalo hides, a horse cost twenty deerskins, and a female slave between twelve and twenty years old cost two good horses and some clothing or woven saddle blankets. Corn was exchanged directly for meat. Colonists also bartered among themselves with chile, *punche* (tobacco), sheep, and other products and animals, which were exchanged for services, goods, and even land.

By 1790, the colonial government may have been making some attempt at economic development, for the census mentions twenty-five *obrajeros* in Santa Fe. An *obraje* was a sweatshop that hired people to weave or produce other articles for sale. In the seventeenth century, sweatshops using Indian labor and run by the Franciscan friars supported the missions. Using forced Indian

New Mexico farmers husking corn.

labor, some governors also ran *obrajes* for their own benefit. *Obrajes* survived for a short time into the eighteenth century, died out, revived towards the end of the century, and then died out again.

Eighteenth-century Santa Fe was a socially stratified society. The governor and his staff of high-ranking officials, along with the officers of the presidio, belonged to the top echelon. The Franciscan clergy in Santa Fe, although seen as a separate group as men of the cloth, were also included at this level of society. But as members of a religious order that stressed the virtue of humility, most friars did not aspire to social prominence. Also, the province had no bishop to create a real hierarchy among the clergy. When Santiago Roybal, New Mexico's first native-born clergyman, was stationed in Santa Fe as vicar and as the local ecclesiastical judge for the diocese of Durango in 1730, he was considered a member of the upper level of society, but the native clergy did not really develop until the nineteenth century.

The next social level consisted of farmers and artisans who were relatively better off than their peers. Then came the common people, with little or no social prominence. The soldiers of the presidio, another separate group, had no special social privileges. In fact, judging from their complaints, they were a poverty-stricken lot whose pay was usually late, and when it did arrive, it went directly to their creditors.

The *Casta* System

Like Spain's other colonial settlements, the population of Santa Fe was multiethnic, as it had been since its founding, and social distinctions often broke along racial lines. The term *casta*, broadly defined as a person of mixed blood, referred to the people of eighteenth-century Santa Fe who were not considered *españoles*—that is, who were not credited with pure Spanish blood, or *pureza de sangre española*.

After King Ferdinand and Queen Isabella's expulsion of the Moors and national unification in 1492, Spaniards began to think of themselves as *españoles* for the first time. Previously, Spain had been divided, not just between Spaniards and Moors, but also among their own petty kingdoms (*patrias chicas*) such as Castile, Leon, and Aragon. The *españoles* began viewing themselves as members of a single nation while still preserving some loyalty to their respective regions. The new spirit of Spanish nationalism was accompanied by an affirmation of Roman Catholicism, which became the state religion. The *españoles* had been fighting not only to regain their peninsula, but also to cast the "infidel Moslems" out of Christian lands. The Catholic religion called for militancy, and the *españoles* saw themselves as defenders and propagators of the Holy Faith (*Santa Fe*).

Religious militancy led to the persecution of non-Christians in Spain, as it had in most European countries up to that time. Jews became special victims of this fervor. The *españoles* never forgot that the Jews had signed a pact with the Moors when they invaded the peninsula and formed cadres in certain towns. The year 1492 witnessed the beginning of a policy to expel Jews who would not convert to Christianity. When many of the Jews converted rather than leave Spain, some of the *españoles* still regarded them with suspicion or condescension, and they were recognized as not being *"de pura sangre española."* Thus the consciousness of *pureza de sangre* was born among Christian Spaniards. The Jews who converted suffered from the stigma of being New Christians, a distinction that gave rise to a new status group, *cristianos viejos*, or Old Christians. The elite among the *españoles*, then, were *"cristianos viejos y de pureza de sangre."* The persistent idea that some of the families who colonized Santa Fe and other areas of New Mexico were descendants of converted Jews has not been documented.

Casta illustration.

In the sixteenth and seventeenth centuries, *españoles* brought the concept of *pureza de sangre* with them to the New World, where they found themselves facing a new social reality—miscegenation. They intermarried with Aztecs, Tlascalans, and other tribes of Mexico, producing offspring who went on to mix further with *españoles* or Indians. To complicate matters, late in the sixteenth century, a new Spanish law forbid the use of Indians for forced labor. When New Spain began importing African slaves to work the mines and do other labor, blacks also began to contribute to the developing genetic pool.

Women at Rancho de las Golondrinas, a Spanish colonial museum near Santa Fe, reenact household chores as they were done in the eighteenth century.

Some blacks did come to the colonies as free men and women, but they were very much in the minority.

By the seventeenth century, a social system for classifying New World ethnic mixtures was evolving. One's social position was determined by the degree of *pureza de sangre española* that flowed in one's veins. To have been born in Spain, especially in Castile, gave one the highest classification possible— *peninsular*. Pure *españoles* who had been born in the New World had the marginally lower status of *criollos* (creoles). The more prestigious offices of government were usually given to *peninsulares* and *criollos*.

Within the growing mixed-blood population, the pecking order was determined by the degree of Spanish blood one possessed, or whether one was pure Indian or black. Indians, especially if Christianized, were of higher status than blacks. In an attempt to make sense of all of this mixing and crossmixing, the *españoles* developed complex racial categories. People who belonged to any of these mixed-blood categories were members of the *castas*. To help colonists understand the *castas*, illustrators depicted the characteristics of each pairing and their offspring.

The 1790 census of Santa Fe recognized six categories of *castas* (Table 1). *Color quebrado* (literally, "broken color") sometimes replaced the wider range of classifications that appeared on typical *casta* lists of the day (Table 2), perhaps because the census taker did not want to do a complete genealogy or just did not believe in the *casta* system. Most of the people living in Barrio de Analco were listed as *color quebrado*, and most of the residents on the plaza side of the river as *españoles*.

In New Mexico, the term *genízaro*, used differently in the rest of the Spanish colonial world, meant a full-blooded Indian who had been captured at a young age by warring Plains Indian tribes and sold to Spanish colonists. *Genízaros* benefitted the colonists economically, for they represented cheap labor in a labor-intensive society. These children, raised as *criados* (servants) in Spanish households, took the names of their Spanish families and went on to start their own families under those names. Well-to-do and poor families

Table 1. The Population of Santa Fe in 1790 *

Category	Male	Percent	Female	Percent
Españoles	820	67.38	875	66.04
Color quebrado	185	15.20	195	14.72
Mestizo	101	8.30	121	9.13
Mulato	42	3.45	43	3.25
Genízaro	31	2.55	5	0.38
Indio	36	2.96	85	6.42
Coyote	2	0.16	1	0.08
Total	1,217		1,325	

Note: These figures do not include the presidio, which numbered about ninety-five soldiers.

alike had *criados*. The Franciscan friars advocated the purchase of these young people to bring them to Christianity.

The census takers also used *genízaro* to mean "civilized Indians who were not Pueblo." Friar Domínguez recorded that forty-two families of *genízaros*, comprised of 164 persons, lived in Santa Fe in 1776, but by 1790, only thirty-six were listed. Friar Morfi, Domínguez's superior, cajoled the governor into giving *genízaros* land of their own so that they would lead independent and productive lives. During this time, New Mexico governors planned to settle *genízaro* families in outlying communities as shock troops, and although the plan was not successful, it may partially account for the decrease in their numbers in Santa Fe. Also, former *genízaros* may have been listed under the general term, *color quebrado*, in 1790.

Casta illustration.

---

* Janie Louise Aragon, "The People of Santa Fe in the 1790s," *Aztlan: International Journal of Chicano Studies Research* 7, no. 3, (1976): 397.

<table>
<tr><td>

Typical Eighteenth-Century *Casta* List *

NON-CASTAS

1. Español
2. Criollo
3. Other Europeans

CASTAS

1. Español x india = mestizo[1]
2. Español x mestiza = castizo[1]
3. Español x castiza = torna a español
4. Español x negra = mulato[1]
5. Español x mulata = morisco
6. Morisco x española = tornatrás
7. Albino x española = tornatrás
8. Mulato x india = calpamulato
9. Negro x india = lobo[1]
10. Lobo x india = cambijo
11. Calpamulato x india = jivaro
12. Indio x cambija = sambahigo
13. Mulato x mestiza = cuarterón
14. Cuarterón x mestiza = coyote[1]
15. Coyote x morisca = albarazado
16. Albarazado x saltatrás = tente en el aire
17. Mestizo x india = cholo
18. Indio x mulata = chino[1]
19. Español x china = cuarterón de china
20. Negro x india = sambo de indio
21. Negro x mulata = genízaro[2]
22. Cambijo x china = genízaro[2]

</td></tr>
</table>

Coyote, also used differently in New Mexico than in the rest of Latin America, seems to have been used almost interchangeably with *mestizo*. Both terms referred to people of mixed Hispanic and Indian blood. It may well be that *coyote* denoted someone who had not achieved the social status of a *mestizo* as defined in Mexico, but who was considered to be of an acceptable *casta* in New Mexico.

It is surprising that 66 percent of the population of Santa Fe in 1790 was classified as *españoles*, high compared to other provinces in New Spain. Undoubtedly, some Santa Fe families were pure *criollo*, and a few were even *peninsulares*. However, it is also possible that some of the people listed as *españoles* were actually *mestizos* who had earned enough distinction politically and financially to be promoted. Domínguez alluded to this possibility by mentioning that some New Mexico citizens "passed" for *españoles*.

The *casta* classification was not as strictly enforced in the frontier provinces as it was in the interior of New Spain. Because *españoles* stood at the top of the social ladder, it seems logical that many would aspire to achieve that category if the social system allowed it. Likewise, the descendants of blacks or *mulatos*, at the bottom of the social scale, may have striven to improve their social condition by working their way into the *color quebrado* category, or even better, that of *mestizo*.

For a *casta*, social acceptance was one thing, but being able to hold high office was quite another. No *casta* ever became governor during this period, for example, or was ordained as a priest to say mass or dispense the sacraments. The attitude of the civil and ecclesiastical authorities was that a *casta* would not be respected by the people and that he might even lapse into a primitive (*cimarrón*) state and cause a scandal. Among farmers, muleteers, shoemakers, and carpenters, however, the common hardships of the frontier served as a

---

* Pedro Alonzo O'Crouley, *A Description of the Kingdom of New Spain, 1774*, translated by Sean Galvin. (San Francisco: John Howell, 1972), 19.

[1] These *castas* are mentioned in the documents pertaining to New Mexico. In New Mexico, *mestizo* or *español* x *india* = *coyote*.

[2] In New Mexico, as explained in the text, the term was used differently.

Santa Fe, July, 1776. Painting by Wilson Hurley, from map by Joseph de Urrutia.

Eighteenth-century Segesser hide painting depicting the Pedro de Villasur expedition to eastern Nebraska. Painting shows Spanish troops and Pueblo Indian auxilliaries being attacked by Pawnee and Oto Indians on August 14, 1720.

social equalizer, and there seems to have been little ethnic discrimination in such occupations.

In the meting out of justice, *españoles* received more lenient sentences than *castas*. For example, *españoles* caught trading with the Utes without government permission were fined ten pesos and their goods were confiscated, but *castas* and *indios* caught breaking the same law were given ten lashes in addition.

Like New Mexico's other settlements, La Villa de Santa Fe struggled to survive during the 1700s. Its only advantage was that as the capital of the province, it had a higher official and social standing. Its citizens were in closer contact with government operations and could enjoy watching the militia going and returning from military operations in the field. Later writers would romanticize Santa Fe's history and its beautiful physical setting. The eighteenth-century citizens of the villa certainly appreciated the beauty of their surroundings, but they would not have made any sense of later romantic notions about their lives as *conquistadores*. By the nineteenth century, the dream of wealth and empire was dead. Whatever their ancestry and social standing, the people of Santa Fe had set their roots deep in a harsh, marginal land. Their lives there had grounded them in a practical approach to life and laid the foundation for their descendants to meet new challenges in the years ahead.

NO.173

East De Vargas Street in the Mexican period probably closely resembled this 1884 photograph.

When Santa Fe Was a Mexican Town

1821 to 1846

JANET LECOMPTE

When Santa Fe was a Mexican town it had a population of only about five thousand, but it was the provincial capital of a huge area that included all of present New Mexico and Arizona and parts of Colorado and Utah. In former centuries the center of town was the presidio, with barracks for a hundred federal soldiers and a large parade ground extending from present Palace Avenue to Federal Place and from Washington Street to Grant Avenue. By the Mexican period only a few soldiers lived in the presidio, much of which was in ruins. The military commander complained that the foundations of the dilapidated barracks were being destroyed by stray chickens, cows, horses, and donkeys. The city council discussed selling the remaining adobe bricks of La Muralla, the wall that surrounded the presidio, to raise a little revenue, for most of the bricks had already been hauled off by townspeople to make new structures.

The Palace of the Governors formed the south side of the presidio. Its west end, where the Museum of Fine Arts now stands, had been lopped off during colonial times, reducing the size of the palace by nearly a third. It was still a long adobe rectangle with a flat roof, shaded on the south by a *portal* (portico) supported by pine pillars. The walk under the *portal*, where Pueblo Indians now sell their wares, was used for a public meeting place and led to the market at the west end of the palace. The adobe palace was often in disrepair. Throughout the seventeenth and eighteenth centuries it was patched and propped up, and its interior partitions were rearranged. In Mexican times it housed the quartermaster, commissariat, and other civil offices, a granary for

The La Castrense *reredos,* or altar piece, presently at the Church of Cristo Rey.

tithes paid in grain, a warehouse for confiscated merchandise, the customs house, the jail, and the guardhouse. It also provided a meeting room for the Provincial Deputation (later the Departmental Assembly) and an office and private quarters for the governor's family.

The man who spent the most time in the palace during the Mexican period was Governor Manuel Armijo. His office was described as a small, plain room about sixteen feet square with two calico-covered sofas against the walls. The floor was covered with a cheap homespun carpet, and the governor's desk was a small table in the center of the room with four crude chairs around it. On the walls were a bill of lading from an American steamship company and dinner plates of various American manufacturers, indicating the governor's interest in trade with the United States.

Downtown Santa Fe

South of the palace was the town plaza. Originally it had been twice as large as it was in the Mexican period. For most of its history the plaza was a rectangle of sunbaked mud where traders parked their wagons and animals, and visiting Indians camped. In the 1820s Governor Antonio Narbona built a rock sundial on an adobe base about eight feet high in the center of the plaza. The sundial bore a Latin inscription, *"Vita fugit sicut umbra"* ("Life flees like a shadow"), and like a shadow it disappeared before 1832, probably knocked down by traders' wagons.

One-story adobe buildings surrounded the plaza. On the east side were government offices, private homes, and a squalid, ruined house where the town council met. On the south side (San Francisco Street) were adobe houses and stores rented in the summer by American traders and the military chapel of La Castrense, considered the handsomest building in town. It was decorated with Spanish paintings brought from Cadiz in 1812 by Don Pedro Pino, the only delegate from New Mexico ever to attend the Spanish Cortes, or national assembly. La Castrense's exquisite altar piece was saved and now adorns the Church of Cristo Rey at the top of Canyon Road. Governor Armijo used to march his presidial soldiers across the plaza to attend services at La Castrense once a week, but by 1846 the chapel was in ruins.

Buildings on the west side of the plaza included Don Juan Vigil's house and his beautiful chapel of the Holy Trinity, which an observer distinguished from other Santa Fe buildings as "immaculate." At the east end of San Francisco Street stood the adobe *parroquia*, or parish church. It was the third church to occupy that spot since the early seventeenth century and was replaced by Bishop Lamy in 1869 with the present stone cathedral. The *parroquia* had faced the plaza before the latter was reduced to its present size in colonial times.

In the Mexican period, Santa Fe was divided into seven districts, each named for a parish church or other familiar landmark. These landmarks were old when New Spain became part of Mexico in 1821, and some are still standing. The district of San Francisco surrounded the *parroquia* and included the plaza and governor's palace. The district of San Miguel centered on the old Indian settlement of Analco surrounding San Miguel Church, now known to tourists as the "oldest church" in the United States. The district of Nuestra Señora de Guadalupe was named for the adobe Guadalupe Church, later demolished and rebuilt in stone by Bishop Lamy. La Muralla district, referring to the remains of the old presidio wall, included Calle de la Muralla (present Washington Street). The road to Albuquerque ran through the district of Agua Fria, as it still does.

Santa Fe during the Mexican period had little of the charm it has today. American visitors called it squalid and ugly, and contemporary records confirm their judgement. Minutes of its *ayuntamiento* (town council) meetings describe dusty streets obstructed with rocks and holes and fouled with piles of garbage thrown from houses. Council members complained that public health was threatened by stagnant pools and undrained marshes and by animal excrement and dead dogs floating in irrigation ditches. At night, vagrants, drunks, and wayward children roamed the streets, as well as traveling strangers whose business was unknown and therefore suspect. Often the silence was shattered by

The *parroquia*, or parish church, stood at the site of the present-day St. Francis Cathedral.

A Santa Fe fandango.

the whoops and yells of revelers at *fandangos* (informal dance parties) and by the ominous crack of American rifles.

Santa Fe's streets were probably no dirtier than those of Mexico City, and much safer. The people of Santa Fe, with a few exceptions, had never seen the streets of a real city with its beggars, criminals, abandoned children, the deformed, and the insane. Santa Fe took care of its own marginal people within its capacious family structures; no one remained homeless or hungry for long.

The People of Santa Fe

Before American traders arrived with their goods, the people of Santa Fe were mostly self sufficient. They built their houses of adobe bricks, using pine beams to hold up the flat roofs, sheets of mica for window lights, and leather for hinges. Few of their houses had tables, chairs, or bedsteads. They spread mattresses on the floor at night and rolled them up against the walls to serve as settees during the day. Their hard earth floors were covered with homemade *jerga*, a coarse woven fabric so inexpensive that traders used it to wrap bales of goods.

Their clothing was simple. Men wore pantaloons of leather or cotton, with plain homespun shirts. Women wore short, full skirts and full, low-necked blouses, with *rebosos* (shawls) over their heads and shoulders. Before the Americans came, New Mexicans imported a few expensive manufacturered goods from Mexico—sugar, shoes, fine cottons, and iron—but their land and labor provided them with everything else.

The people of Santa Fe valued honesty, generosity, hospitality, courtesy, loyalty to one's family and community, and obedience to authority when it did not conflict with their passionate individualism. They worked no harder than completion of the task required, and they lightened their labor by working with others, sometimes making a joyous game of it. Social occasions such as church festivals, weddings, and nightly *fandangos* were fully attended, for New Mexicans were a gregarious people.

The Mexican period began in the spring of 1821, when revolutionaries in Mexico set up a republic independent of the Kingdom of Spain. Because Santa Fe was located 1,600 miles north of Mexico, its people did not hear of the new government until September 11, when a horseman arrived with a mail pouch of official correspondence demanding that New Mexico's governor and other officials take an oath of allegiance. The people of Santa Fe received the news calmly. As a sequestered colony of Spain, New Mexico had been isolated for centuries from the rest of the world, and her people had little understanding of what a republic was.

In their isolation, New Mexicans had assumed a degree of local autonomy and a habit of resistance to central control. When in October the government sent a decree ordering New Mexicans to celebrate independence immediately, the people complied, but not until January. Their celebration included processions, orations, patriotic dramas, music, masses, ringing of church bells, firing of muskets, dancing of Pueblo Indians, and a ball in the governor's palace. Governor Melgares reported that the celebration was a very genteel affair and just what the government had ordered, but an American visitor described the street celebration as "licentiousness of every description," with crowds of gamblers enjoying "unrestrained vice" at dice and faro tables. Gambling, though illegal, was described as "the national sport of Mexico."

In 1821 Americans were trading with Indians on the borders of New Mexico. When they heard that Mexico's new government welcomed foreign commerce, as Spain had not, they entered Santa Fe and sold their goods quickly. By early 1822 William Becknell had already returned to Missouri for more goods to bring along the Santa Fe Trail. The trade between Missouri and Santa Fe was, in the end, the most signficant result of Mexican independence for New Mexico. At first, Americans and their goods were not much more than a diversion in Santa Fe. On Sundays after church people gathered in the plaza to shop, drink, dance, and gamble. Along San Francisco Street and around the plaza American traders rented stores to sell their calicos and muslins to the natives, and the natives responded by opening wineshops and monte tables for Americans.

Mexican girls.

Before long Americans and their goods had altered many aspects of everyday life in Santa Fe. Most rooms now had dadoes of calicos and ginghams, a profusion of American mirrors on the bare, whitewashed interior walls, and an occasional clock or piece of American furniture. For special occasions women put aside their peasant blouses and skirts to appear at balls in tight-waisted American gowns, and men who wore homespun shirts, buckskin breeches, and moccasins for work, dressed up in muslin shirts, imported trousers, and boots. Besides luxuries, traders' imports included useful things such as tools, medicines, newspapers, primers for schools, and a printing press. Some Americans built distilleries and made whiskey from wheat grown in the Taos Valley; others had sawmills or flour mills, or practiced their skills as carpenters, trappers, hatters, surveyors, gunsmiths, and blacksmiths, and taught these skills to New Mexicans.

Americans became indispensable, not only for their goods and skills, but also for the customs duties they paid, which supported both the civil officers of the territory and the presidial soldiers. Some Americans became citizens and lifelong residents, serving in municipal offices and as valued advisors to the governors. Many volunteered to fight Indians in the citizen-militia. Americans loaned money to the New Mexico treasury when it was empty and set up schemes for profit that further enriched the rich men of Santa Fe and provided jobs for the poor.

Although some Americans became respected citizens of New Mexico, others were arrogant and lawless. American hunters trapped beaver illegally in Mexican streams from New Mexico to California and south into Chihuahua and Sonora. American merchants cheated their customers with short weights and measures and sold guns to Indians. Traders smuggled in contraband goods and filled their wagons, returning to Missouri with contraband gold and silver bullion, specie, and illegal beaver pelts. In a land where courtesy was the first rule of conduct, Americans were often rude. They jeered at New Mexican folkways, broke up *fandangos* with drunken violence, and seduced and then abandoned both wives and maidens.

West San Francisco Street in 1881.

American trapper.

For better or worse, Americans influenced the lives and thoughts of New Mexicans. Contemporary Mexicans observed that the American work ethic, with its emphasis on accumulation of land and capital, began to undermine the leisurely quality of New Mexican life. American-style liberty and independence made some New Mexicans critical of their government and church and eager to choose their own political parties and leaders, as we shall see in the rebellion of 1837. Mexicans' perceptions of American wealth, freedom, and power was a factor in the ease with which Colonel Stephen W. Kearny conquered New Mexico in 1846. The cultural and ideological contributions of Americans were more influential in New Mexico than all the confused policies of the failed Mexican republic.

Nevertheless, it would be an error to assume that New Mexicans did not already have freedoms similar to those that Americans enjoyed. The constitutional government that the Republic of Mexico adopted in 1824 provided for a national congress of representatives from states and territories and citizenship for both Indians and blacks, although not for criminals and women. The 1824 constitution was modeled on that of the United States in its provisions for free trade and free speech, but in other ways it was different. It tolerated only the Roman Catholic Church, and it promised laws for New Mexico and other territories that were never promulgated. Through much of the Mexican period, New Mexican officials were forced to use Spanish laws passed by the Cortes of 1812, with suitable and often arbitrary changes to fit local conditions.

The governor (*jefe político*) was often made military chief as well. He was appointed by the president of Mexico with consent of the Mexican Congress, as were the secretary, treasurer, district judge, and *asesor* (legal advisor to the government). The latter two positions were rarely filled in New Mexico for lack of qualified men. The Territorial Deputation or Assembly consisted of seven men who met in Santa Fe and acted upon territorial matters, including the choice of a deputy to the Mexican Congress. The town council consisted of unpaid citizens who passed local ordinances and elected an alcalde to serve as its chairman and as mayor and municipal judge.

One of the permanent changes made by the Republic of Mexico was the abolishment of the old Spanish caste system, based on supposed degree of Hispanic blood. Now every respectable man could hold the title of "don," and native New Mexicans replaced Spanish knights as governors.

Governor Manuel Armijo

Manuel Armijo was the best known of the Mexican governors of New Mexico, and he was no Spanish knight. Born into a rich Albuquerque family in 1793, a mestizo of Spanish, Mexican Indian, and Plains Indian stock, he grew up to be handsome and portly, arrogant and charming, quick tempered and tough. Although he served three separate terms (1827–29, 1837–44, and 1845–46) and proved to be a fine administrator and clever politician, he was not popular, especially with Americans. Two contemporary American writers, Josiah Gregg and George Wilkins Kendall, both published books about New Mexico in 1844 portraying Armijo as a tyrant, a monster of lust and greed, an enemy to Americans, and a coward. Their best-selling books established a reputation for Armijo that was worse than he deserved.

Governor Armijo was hated by Americans for, among other things, his hostile confrontations with their well-armed countrymen. In 1827, during his first term as governor, he was determined to stop illegal fur trapping by Americans in Mexican territory. One day American trappers impudently cleaned their contraband beaver pelts in the plaza in front of the governor's palace, in full view of all Santa Fe. Armijo ordered his guard to seize the furs and arrest the trappers, but when the trappers began loading their guns, Armijo became uneasy and ordered the guard to retreat. The trappers escaped with their furs and jeered Armijo as a coward.

Armijo and other Santa Fe officials had good cause to fear armed Americans. In all New Mexico there were probably no more than 250 operable muskets, and usually fewer than 100 trained presidial soldiers. The hundreds of frontiersmen accompanying a single American caravan (such as the 1843 caravan of 230 wagons) would have had more and better guns than all New

General Manuel Armijo.

José Antonio Laureano de Zubiría, bishop of Durango.

Mexicans put together, and far more skill in using them. It was possible that a caravan of traders with their superior guns could have caught Santa Fe unawares and captured the city—or so Armijo feared. The governor and other responsible men of New Mexico continually warned the central government of the possibility of foreign invasion, and begged in vain for more money, soldiers, arms, and ammunition.

Armijo's fears were vindicated when 350 well-armed Texans arrived on New Mexico's eastern border in 1841 to capture Santa Fe in the name of the Republic of Texas, then at war with Mexico. Armijo met them on the eastern frontier, professed friendship, and persuaded them to lay down their arms. Without their guns the Texans were helpless. Armijo tied them together and sent them on foot to Mexico for the disposition of the president.

The Republic in Disarray

In this emergency and others, the central government of Mexico was powerless to help New Mexico, for its own affairs were in chaos. Between 1821 and 1837 the presidency turned over twenty-seven times, often violently. With such turmoil at the center, the outlying provinces suffered neglect and privation. Santa Fe showed the strain of poverty in its institutions, its buildings, and in the frustrations of its people. At one point the assembly disbanded for lack of travel money, and government offices closed for lack of paper, ink, and wood for heating the rooms in winter. In 1833 the government withdrew its support for churches and clergy. Henceforth the old churches, built by Franciscan friars with Indian labor in past centuries, were maintained only by donations. The buildings became dilapidated, their sacramental linens threadbare, their silver plate dented and tarnished, and their vestments shabby. Franciscan priests became scarce. Most of them were natives of Spain, and in 1827, during a quarrel with Spain, Mexico banished Spanish-born citizens. During the Mexican period only five to eight secular priests remained in New Mexico, far too few to administer sacraments to all the people.

No bishop visited New Mexico between 1760 and 1833. Confirmations all but ceased for half a century, baptisms decreased in number, and couples lived together without benefit of marriage. When Bishop Zubiría finally made the journey to Santa Fe from his diocese in Durango in 1833, the people were overjoyed. They sprinkled the streets with water to keep down the dust, constructed arbors of pine branches over the route of the episcopal procession, whitewashed buildings, and decorated bridges that would meet His Worship's eyes. The results of the bishop's visit were hardly worth the trouble of cleaning up Santa Fe. After administering sacraments and tendering his blessings, he departed, but not before offending everyone by outlawing the *penitentes*. This lay brotherhood provided many parishioners of northern New Mexico with their only source of religious ritual and comfort, in the absence of a sufficient number of priests. After the bishop's visit, the church continued to neglect New Mexico as usual, but the *penitentes* thrived.

The military also suffered in the nineteenth century. The 120 presidial troops formerly allotted to New Mexico were sometimes reduced to about 60 in the Mexican period. Their uniforms were tattered and incomplete, lacking hats, coats, or jackets. A few were armed with ancient and barely serviceable muskets and scanty ammunition, but most had only clubs, lances, or bows and arrows. The soldiers were entitled to succor (provisions and shelter) and a salary, usually paid in grain. Some were owed twenty years' pay but remained in service for lack of land or other employment. They were drilled in European maneuvers and drawn battle lines, making their training useless against the hit-and-run warfare of Indians.

As their numbers declined in the Mexican period, the presidial troop served only to lead American caravans into Santa Fe to prevent smuggling, to escort the mail through Indian country, and to provide a ceremonial guard for the governor. They also served as Santa Fe's police, performing such degrading duties as killing stray dogs on the streets and flushing gamblers out of private homes in the dead of night.

The real soldiers of New Mexico were its ragtag militiamen, sometimes commanded by officers of the presidial troop, who fought in the miserable

New Mexico *penitentes,* circa 1890–96.

Life on Santa Fe's plaza in the nineteenth century.

campaigns against Navajos and Apaches in the 1830s. Militia were requisitioned by the alcalde; they received no succor or salary, and they furnished their own arms, mounts, and provisions for three-month enlistments. As paltry compensation, they shared the spoils captured in battle. Rich men often paid poor men to substitute for them in the militia, but even so, the expense of campaigns often ruined the small farmers and Pueblo Indians who composed it.

The Society of Mexican Santa Fe

In previous centuries, New Mexico had been in constant danger from hostile Indians. Government aid was rarely forthcoming, and citizens of all classes were forced to pool their efforts to survive. Consequently, New Mexico developed its own version of a democratic society and a spirit of independence unique to the frontier. In Santa Fe, the stratifications of society were blurred, at least on social occasions. At Governor Armijo's ball at the palace in 1839, an American reported, "All the beauty and fashion attended and all the rabble, for, true to their republican principles, none can be refused admission." Another wrote, "It was not anything uncommon or surprising to see the most elaborately dressed and aristocratic women at the ball dancing with a peon dressed only in his shirt and trousers."

By virtue of Spanish and Indian tradition and the influence of the frontier, the independence of New Mexicans was especially apparent in their women. Every Sunday after church, women gathered in the plaza to sell vegetables, cheese, and American whiskey, or to deal cards in games of monte. Women had their own businesses and were not required to turn profits over to their husbands, as they were in the United States. They could own rental property such as a house or a billiard table, and they owned flocks of sheep which they entrusted to a shepherd in return for a percentage of the lamb crop.

The most famous woman in Santa Fe was Gertrudes Barcelo, known as La Tules. In the 1830s and 1840s she ran a bar and gambling casino that stretched the length of Burro Alley. Although not beautiful, she was a very bright, witty, and elegant woman, "the height of fashion," wrote one American. She was said to be Governor Armijo's mistress; at the least she was his close friend and advisor. She became so rich that after the occupation of Santa Fe she loaned money to the United States Army to pay its soldiers.

In an era when most wives of the world were mere chattels of their husbands, married women of Santa Fe kept their own wages and their maiden names. Their legal rights were such that they could even sue their husbands. Women also enjoyed sexual freedom. During the Mexican period fewer than half the couples of Santa Fe were married. Men and women lived together and raised children in relationships sanctified by society if not by the church.

Another independent group were the *genízaros*, Plains Indians captured as children and brought up as Mexicans in Mexican communities. In the nineteenth century they were allowed their own settlements and government; the towns of San Miguel and Abiquiu were first populated by *genízaros*. In Santa Fe, *genízaros* settled in Barrio de Analco with descendants of Indians brought from Mexico as servants of early Spaniards. They were finally absorbed into the mestizo population.

Although the citizens of New Mexico were generally patriotic, docile, and obedient, New Mexico's officials often acted independently of the central government, ignoring federal laws and edicts when they were not in the best interests of New Mexico. For instance, Governor Armijo refused to obey an order from the central government to make war against the Comanches because the tribe was at peace with the people of New Mexico. This notoriously independent governor exceeded the rights of his office by hearing appeals from dissatisfied litigants in the alcalde courts because there was no judge in New Mexico. New Mexico received no money from the central government for public works—roads, bridges, hospitals, and schools. Its presidial soldiers were paid out of customs house receipts that the national government allowed Santa Fe to keep, but when customs receipts were low, the soldiers were dismissed. The people paid no federal income or property taxes in New Mexico, however, in acknowledgment of their militia service on the frontier.

La Doña Tules

Mexico's neglect of New Mexico was symptomatic of that government's failure, and by the mid-1830s the Republic of Mexico was plainly not working well at the center. In 1835 conservatives drew up a new constitution dividing the country into departments with governors directly responsible to the president. All departments were to be governed alike, with autonomy for none and taxes for all. The departments that suffered most were those farthest from central Mexico, and many of them rebelled, including New Mexico.

In 1835 the central government appointed Albino Pérez as governor of New Mexico to put centralism and taxation into operation. New Mexicans disliked not only the new policies but also the new governor, who was handsome and brave but entirely too sophisticated for them. He did not bother to conceal his taste for luxuries—fur capes and fancy clothes, silver-mounted saddles and camp chairs, an imported American carriage, and a Santa Fe mistress in the absence of his wife in Mexico. During his governorship the plainly furnished palace was filled with extravagances such as gilded mirrors, a large table clock, and calico-covered sofas. Pérez gathered sycophants about him and amassed debts he could not pay.

Angry at the excesses of the new governor and the threat of taxes, men of the northern part of New Mexico sought to throw out the new constitution and establish a popular government. They formed a mob that savagely murdered seventeen civil and military officers, including Governor Pérez. The rebels then occupied Santa Fe, camping in the open field near the Rosario Chapel. As governor they elected one of their own, José Gonzáles, a simple, honest, illiterate man. While Gonzáles occupied the governor's palace and tried to bring tranquility to Santa Fe, secret plans were being made to get rid of the unruly rebels. In the town of Tomé, near Albuquerque, former governor Manuel Armijo organized a small army, marched to Santa Fe, and persuaded the rebels to go home. Then Armijo executed the leaders of the rebellion and assumed the governorship. Early in 1838 he was confirmed in the office and prepared to serve his second term as governor.

Armijo was a good governor. From 1838 to 1843 he worked to reduce the department's debt to soldiers, civil servants, and Americans who had loaned money to put down the revolution. He constantly badgered the central government for money, soldiers, and guns, defying directives and laws that did not meet the needs of New Mexico. By 1841 he had reduced depredations of the Navajos and made a treaty with them that was at least partly effective. He supported the demoralized priests and ordered parishioners to help repair and clean up their churches. He also encouraged teachers and wrote often on the people's need for literacy.

Armijo recognized the American traders as the economic salvation of New Mexico. In 1839 he illegally lowered duties on goods imported from the United States. The number of American traders multiplied, as did customs duties, and the financial state of the department improved. He also made illegal concessions to Mexican merchants, increasing their participation in the Santa Fe trade to the extent that Mexican wagons along the Santa Fe Trail outnumbered those of Americans by 1843.

Then Armijo made an error that ended his second term as governor. In 1843 he led an army of citizens against Texan pirates gathered on the Arkansas River to the north, but at the first danger of confrontation, he ordered a retreat. His cowardice was duly reported to Mexico, and he was ordered to give up his military command. Early in 1844 he resigned his civil office as well and retired to his home in Albuquerque.

Armijo was replaced by General Mariano Martínez de Lejanza, a man from central Mexico with good intentions and military experience. But like Governor Pérez, Martínez de Lejanza was not familiar with the people and problems of New Mexico, and he made mistakes. During an argument with some Ute Indian allies in the reception room of the palace, he hit one of the chiefs with a chair. The chief died, and the Utes began a war with New Mexico. Martínez de Lejanza also raised customs duties, to the detriment of the Santa Fe trade, and infuriated the people by trying to collect direct taxes. He was recalled to Mexico, and his only memorial in New Mexico were the cottonwood trees he had planted in the Santa Fe plaza.

Monument to Governor Albino Pérez on Agua Fria Street, since moved to the patio of the Palace of the Governors.

Burro Alley, circa 1895–98.

In November 1845 Manuel Armijo began his third, shortest, and last term as governor and military commander of New Mexico. New Mexico received word in June 1846 that the United States had declared war on Mexico a month earlier, putting Armijo in a difficult position. New Mexico's only financial support—its only business—was the Santa Fe trade with Americans. Yet, as a general in the Mexican army, Armijo was obliged to fight Americans if ordered to do so.

On July 7 news arrived in Santa Fe that an American army was camped at Bent's Fort on the Arkansas River, prepared to invade New Mexico. The people were terrified, for their priests had told them that Americans would rape women and brand men on the cheek like cattle. Many families abandoned their homes and fled to the mountains. At Armijo's call to arms, more than 4,000 men from all over gathered in Santa Fe. Frantically, Armijo collected money to succor them, ordering the church to turn over its silver plate and livestock and demanding funds from the city council and Departmental Assembly.

On August 15, as General Stephen W. Kearny and his army marched ever closer, United States agents secretly met Armijo at the palace, begging him to give up New Mexico peacefully. It was said that the agents offered him a bribe, but there is no good evidence of it. Still undecided, Armijo ordered his citizen-army to march out and fortify Apache Canyon, a steep-sided, narrow gap on Kearny's route to Santa Fe. The next day Armijo followed with the presidial troop. At Apache Canyon, he finally made up his mind and ordered the people to return to their homes. He continued south with his presidial troop to meet Mexican forces coming north to defend Santa Fe. In Mexico City Armijo was tried and acquitted of treason. He returned to New Mexico, where he died in 1853.

General Kearny and his army marched into Santa Fe with drawn sabres. They met no opposition, only sullen faces and downcast eyes. The wail of women rose above the din of the horses' hooves. As cannons boomed, soldiers raised the American flag on a newly constructed pole in the plaza. One soldier wrote later that he saw black eyes peering from behind latticed windows, many filled with tears, but a few gleaming with joy. The moment held both despair and hope—sorrow that Santa Fe was no longer a loving child of Spain and Mexico, and anticipation that the United States would prove a more attentive parent.

The American Occupation of Santa Fe

"My Government Will Correct All This"

JOHN P. WILSON

On August 18, 1846, Brigadier General Stephen Watts Kearny led his 1,500-man Army of the West into Santa Fe to claim New Mexico for the United States. Some residents greeted the American occupation of their ancient city with sullen looks and muttered curses, others with winsome smiles. Kearny's troops welcomed the bloodless conquest at the end of their long march, one that climaxed a convoluted series of political events.

Prelude: 1836–1846

For roughly 240 years, the boundaries of New Mexico had generally been set by the most remote line of settlements in the province. In 1819, when New Mexico's frontiers still lay at Taos and the villages along the upper Pecos River, the United States signed a treaty recognizing all of the lands south and west from the Arkansas River as belonging to Spain, and later, to Mexico. Texas complicated this situation in 1836 when it declared independence from Mexico and claimed the Rio Grande to its source, then northward to the forty-second parallel, as a western boundary. The Texas claim, which lacked any historical basis and included half of New Mexico, set the stage for conflict.

New Mexico Governor Manuel Armijo recognized the threat and managed to forestall one invasion from Texas. U.S. dragoons under Captain Philip St. George Cooke disarmed another set of raiders. The president of Mexico reacted by closing the northern ports of entry to commerce, which had the

Opposite page: General Kearny's Army of the West entering Santa Fe plaza, August 18, 1846. Painting by Don Spaulding. Courtesy, Sunswest Bank of Santa Fe.

General Stephen Watts Kearny, circa 1847.

unintended effect of depriving Armijo of his only revenue source, import duties. In mid-January 1844, Armijo resigned as civil governor. For two years, government in New Mexico ranged between confusion and chaos.

The United States meanwhile elected a new president, James K. Polk, who entertained decidedly expansionist views. The United States annexed Texas, and in December of 1845 Texas became a state, with its western boundary designated as the Rio Grande. President Polk's intentions went beyond Texas. He wanted to acquire California as well and squelch any British designs on either area. New Mexico may or may not have been an afterthought, but by September 1845 he was ready to ask for cabinet approval of a plan to settle the claim to Texas and also to "adjust a permanent boundary between Mexico and the United States" by negotiating with Mexico to purchase the country north of a line drawn west from El Paso to the Pacific Ocean. The cabinet agreed unanimously, and in November Polk sent John Slidell as his minister to Mexico with secret instructions to offer a graduated scale of payments for increasing amounts of the country north of the thirty-second parallel.

The Mexican government refused to receive Slidell, who never got to present Polk's proposals; nevertheless, rumors spread to Santa Fe that Mexico had agreed to sell New Mexico to the United States. This garbled story provoked a protest from New Mexico's leading citizens, who denied Mexico's right to sell the province and swore to defend it. Slidell meanwhile reported the Mexican government's refusal to receive him. When this news reached Washington on January 12, 1846, Polk ordered Brigadier General Zachary Taylor to advance his 4,000-man "Army of Observation" from Corpus Christi, Texas, to a point on the disputed boundary along the Rio Grande. With this movement, only a spark was needed to set off a war.

Polk was a president who engaged in brinksmanship. He never explained his strategy, and as a result, several interpretations of the causes for the Mexican War have grown up. One school of thought laid the blame on American territorial ambitions and the desire to provoke a war of conquest against a weak and divided Mexico. Not surprisingly, this theory has had a congenial reception in Mexico. Another thesis placed the onus upon Mexico for its unwillingness to accept the annexation of Texas, a step that by 1846 was irreversible. More recent studies suggest that neither side wanted war, but that Polk's attempts to negotiate a purchase while simultaneously exerting military pressure, combined with his lack of understanding of Mexico and the stresses within it, placed that country in an impossible situation.

For Mexico's leaders to have negotiated and surrendered territory at a time when the country's national existence appeared to be at stake would have ensured a rebellion. A refusal to negotiate was certain to bring on a war that most Mexican officials probably did not want. War, on the other hand, would at least preserve the national honor while providing a means to unite a seriously divided nation and perhaps setting the stage for a series of reforms. In the end neither country adopted a conciliatory position. The Mexicans continued their refusal to receive Slidell, and Polk, seeing no alternative to war, began to plan accordingly. The first overt action, a skirmish between Mexican troops and an American detachment near present-day Brownsville, Texas, took place in late April 1846. It may have come as a relief to both sides.

Slidell reported back to Washington personally on May 8, 1846. One day later, word arrived of the fight between Zachary Taylor's dragoons and some Mexican cavalry. The president drafted a message to Congress, and on May 13, Congress passed an act recognizing the existing war with Mexico and authorizing 50,000 volunteers to fight it. By this time American and Mexican soldiers on the lower Rio Grande had fought three engagements.

New Mexico and the Army of the West

On May 13 the president and the secretary of war directed Colonel Stephen Watts Kearny, stationed at Fort Leavenworth, on the Missouri River, to protect the trade caravans then en route from Missouri to Santa Fe. They also agreed to dispatch a column to seize New Mexico, calling upon the governor of Missouri to raise 1,000 mounted volunteers as a supplement to Kearny's First U.S. Dragoons. As usual the authorities in Santa Fe were well informed; in early June they understood that a war was imminent, and by June 24 at the

Hall's breechloader, type used by Kearny's soldiers.

Kearny's troops crossing the New Mexico mountains. *Opposite page:* map of Santa Fe, 1846–47, by J. F. Gilmore.

latest they had learned that an American army was advancing across the plains from Fort Leavenworth, distant some 856 miles by way of the Santa Fe Trail and Bent's Fort on the Arkansas River.

In fact, Kearny's march to Santa Fe with his Army of the West was based on a plan forwarded to the adjutant general of the army on September 4, 1845. Major Richard B. Lee had recently returned from Santa Fe, and the U.S. War Department solicited detailed information and recommendations from him. Lee's response was a handbook for the conquest of Santa Fe, complete with distances, routes, numbers, the proposed composition of the army itself, rendezvous points, rations, costs, and much more. He recommended only a thousand men in all with a single artillery company (four guns), and naively thought that "by a cautious approach and a night march" his force could advance undetected at least as far as San Miguel del Vado. Indeed, Major Lee mapped out the conquest of New Mexico ten months before it happened. When Kearny set off he had a copy of Lee's report in his pocket.

New Mexico in the spring of 1846 was a province already under attack from the neighboring Ute and Navajo Indians. They raided with impunity, and the frontier settlements were nearly defenseless against their assaults. The local militia lacked horses and weapons, the presidial soldiers had not been paid in a long time, the treasury was empty, and the central government in Mexico offered encouragement but little or no real help.

Manuel Armijo returned to office for his third term as civil governor of New Mexico in November of 1845, and in March 1846 he was appointed commanding general as well. He established a new militia system and organized reconnaissance parties to patrol the frontier regions while making all manner of futile appeals for money to meet New Mexico's urgent financial needs. When his pleas failed, the governor was reduced to issuing proclamations and circulars to stir the national pride.

Under these conditions, it is understandable why the first news about an American army crossing the plains caused great consternation in Santa Fe. It was not clear whether the advancing forces were Texans or Americans, though by this time Armijo was fully aware of the ambitions of the United States and

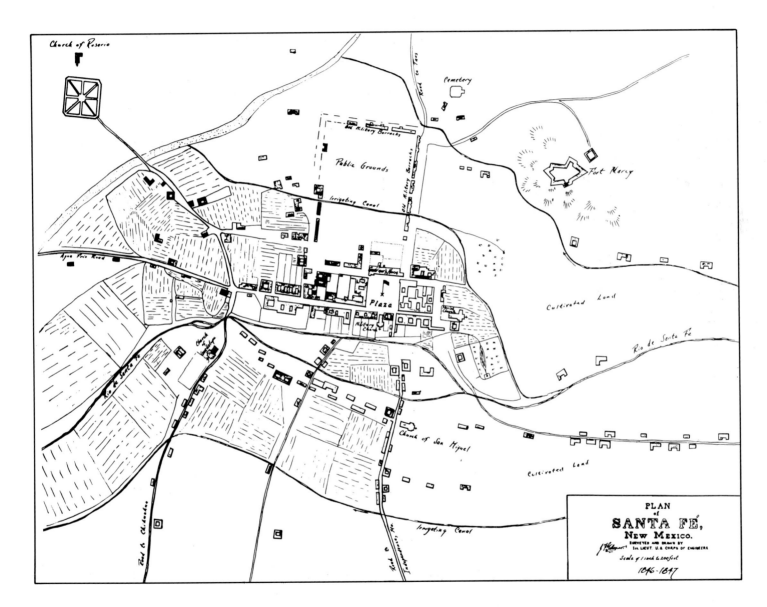

Church of Rosario

Cemetery

Road to Taos

Old Military Barracks

Public Grounds

Irrigating Canal

Old Military Barracks

Fort Marcy

Cultivated Land

Rio de Santa Fe

Agua Fria Road

Plaza

Cultivated Land

Rio de Santa Fe

Church of Guadalupe

Church of San Miguel

Road to Chihuahua

Road to Independence Mo.

Irrigating Canal

PLAN
of
SANTA FÉ,
NEW MEXICO.
SURVEYED AND DRAWN BY
1ST LIEUT. U.S. CORPS OF ENGINEERS
Scale of 1 inch to 200 feet
1846-1847

Colonel Alexander W. Doniphan, 1881–82.

that country's assumption of the Texas claim to the Rio Grande as its boundary with Mexico. Within New Mexico there were mixed sentiments about both Mexican sovereignty and Armijo himself, at least while the enemy remained out of sight. A greater concern lay with the economic consequences of delays in the summer caravan's arrival from Missouri. The forty wagons that finally rolled into the city included the train brought by Albert Speyer, Armijo's business partner, with thousands of pesos worth of goods consigned to the governor. After this, Armijo's decisions heavily favored his personal business interests.

Everything the governor heard during July indicated that the North Americans were coming with no less than 2,500 troops, all well equipped, and accompanied by upwards of twenty-four artillery pieces. Around August 1 or 2 a newly arrived merchant doubled the estimate of the number of American soldiers. Manuel Armijo's 200 regulars and poorly armed, untrained militia would be swept aside by a force of that size. His resolution now wavering, Armijo authorized himself to conduct the annual caravan south to Chihuahua, then drew up a power of attorney giving a trusted friend the authority to settle his affairs in the future. To the public he continued to put up a bold front, but by now it was a bluff. With the Americans only days away he ordered out the militia, bringing to Santa Fe as many as 4,000 citizen-soldiers. He assured them that "your governor is willing and ready to sacrifice his life and all his interests in the defense of his country," but with the moment of truth approaching, Don Manuel had already made his decision to abandon New Mexico.

War preparations were also going on at Fort Leavenworth, near the eastern end of the Santa Fe Trail. The U.S. Army had one of its ablest officers in Colonel Stephen W. Kearny, and in little more than a month he assembled nearly 1,500 men and had them ready to march. Most were volunteers—all Missourians—with Colonel Alexander Doniphan's regiment of First Missouri Mounted Volunteers constituting over half of the force. In addition there were two companies of volunteer infantry, the LaClede Rangers from St. Louis, two companies of artillery (sixteen guns in all), and five companies from Kearny's own First Dragoons. The volunteers began to move out on June 22, 1846, followed by Kearny with his staff and the artillery on June 30. The army required most of July

to march the 537 miles to Bent's Fort, a private trading post on the upper Arkansas River a few miles east of present-day La Junta, Colorado.
Junta, Colorado.

While at Bent's Fort, Kearny issued a proclamation to the citizens of New Mexico, sounding the themes that he was to repeat during the next several weeks. He was entering New Mexico to seek union with its inhabitants and ameliorate their condition. People who remained quietly at their homes would be protected in their rights, both civil and religious. Those who took up arms would be regarded as enemies and dealt with accordingly. Nothing was said about a boundary or any other unresolved differences between Mexico and the United States.

The same day that the Army of the West broke camp at Bent's Fort, Kearny sent Captain Cooke and a prominent Santa Fe trader named James Magoffin on ahead with an escort of dragoons to try and negotiate a peaceful surrender from Governor Armijo. When this party arrived in Santa Fe on August 12, Cooke found the plaza crowded with thousands of soldiers and countrymen called out to resist the American invasion. The envoys' reception was hospitable, nonetheless. Cooke was shown to the governor's palace, where, as he recollected,

> I entered from the hall, a large and lofty apartment, with a carpeted earth floor, and discovered the governor seated at a table, with six or eight military and civil officials standing. There was no mistaking the governor, a large fine looking man. . . . He wore a blue frock coat, with a rolling collar and a general's shoulder straps, blue striped trowsers with gold lace, and a red sash.

Captain Cooke then presented a letter from Kearny stating that by virtue of the annexation of Texas, he had come to take possession of the country. Armijo politely declined to accept this version of events but offered to negotiate. That evening, James Magoffin conferred with General Armijo, and the two men then met secretly with Cooke.

Magoffin never understated his own importance in these negotiations.

Woodcut of Bent's Fort, 1847.

James W. Magoffin.

What he claimed at the time was recorded in the diary kept by Lieutenant William H. Emory, Kearny's chief engineer officer, in a paragraph edited out from the published version of the diary:

> Mr. McGriffin [Magoffin], an American, says that the night Armijo's messenger returned from General Kearny with the news that the latter had refused to stop, but was still advancing, he (Armijo) was thrown into the greatest trepidation: that he sent for him, (Mr. McGriffin), embraced him, and asked him for God's sake to go out and use his influence with General Kearny, to *stop* him. When Mr. McGriffin told him that was impossible, he gave way to the most uncontrollable despair.

On the other hand, there is circumstantial evidence that a bribe was offered and accepted and that Armijo's second-in-command, Colonel Diego Archuleta, was disaffected of his intention to fight the Americans by an offer of control over New Mexico *west* of the Rio Grande. Not for another ten days, on August 22, was anything said publicly about the claim of the United States to lands beyond the river. When Cooke and his party left Santa Fe to return to the army, they may have borne the knowledge that Armijo was not going to fight. They rejoined Kearny two days later at Tecolote, New Mexico.

Accounts of what happened in the New Mexican camp over the next several days are contradictory. Governor Armijo was apparently embarrassed and surprised by the huge turnout his call to arms brought. On August 14 he ordered the throngs of people to leave the city and take up positions at Apache Canyon, fifteen miles to the east. Two days later the general rode out to join his troops, where he convened a junta to decide what to do. The consensus was to fight, but Armijo declined to lead this array and ordered the militia to return to their homes. One young officer later said that there was little choice because the army had no leaders or food supplies and lacked military training. The governor himself fled south to Chihuahua accompanied by seventy of the Vera Cruz dragoons, whom had been sent to help with the defense.

General Kearny (he received his commission at Las Vegas, New Mexico)

Dress parade, Fort Marcy, 1897.

repeated the contents of his earlier proclamation when the Army of the West passed through Las Vegas, Tecolote, and San Miguel del Vado. The alcalde of Pecos rode out to greet them and said, with a roar of laughter, "Armijo and his troops have gone to hell, and the cañon is all clear!" Kearny required the community leaders to take oaths of allegiance and reminded them of the ravages by Apaches and Navajos. His promise, "My government will correct all this," would haunt future military commanders in New Mexico.

On the night of August 17 the Americans camped twenty-nine miles short of Santa Fe, resolved to push on to the capital city the next day. The army broke camp early and pushed on until the head of the column came in sight

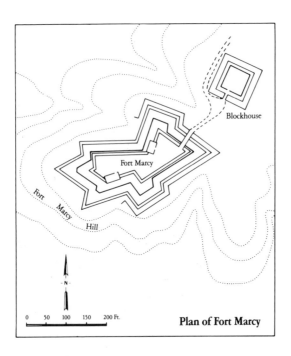

Blockhouse

Fort Marcy

Fort Marcy Hill

N

0   50   100 150   200 Ft.

Plan of Fort Marcy

of the town about three o'clock, the last units arriving around six. They marched through Santa Fe to the governor's palace, where General Kearny and his staff were received by the acting governor, Juan Bautista Vigil y Alarid, and other dignitaries and conducted inside.

Vigil had wine and brandy set out for refreshments. As one officer described it, "During the repast, and as the sun was setting, the United States flag was hoisted over the palace, and a salute of thirteen guns fired from the artillery planted on the eminence overlooking the town." Ceremonies over, the officers were invited to dinner by "a Mexican gentleman," a Captain Ortiz. The dinner "was served very much after the manner of a French dinner, one dish succeeding another in endless variety," all washed down with more wine from El Paso del Norte. Captain Cooke drew provost duty that night, however, and he witnessed the taverns and saloons of Santa Fe being overrun by the hungry and thirsty volunteers until he had to drive them all out.

What did New Mexicans think about this change of national allegiance? A Santa Fe trader told Kearny when he was still east of Bent's Fort that the populace was ready to accept occupation, but not so the leaders. The army's rapid advance had given no one in New Mexico much time to think about what to do, and when confronted with a choice of losing their office or swearing allegiance to the United States, the local alcaldes all took the oath, however reluctantly. In Santa Fe on the morning following the occupation, Kearny once more announced his peaceful intentions and "proclaimed" the people American citizens, subject to a new government. In a graceful response, the acting governor accepted their new situation on behalf of the inhabitants of New Mexico, asking that the general not find it strange if there were no manifestations of joy or enthusiasm.

Three days later General Kearny published a new proclamation, elaborating slightly upon the one he had issued at Bent's Fort and making it clear that he claimed "New Mexico, with its original boundaries (on both sides of the Del Norte) as a part of the United States, under the name of the Territory of New Mexico." This announcement evidently brought little reaction, consistent with the resignation that people had shown thus far. There would be serious trouble later, but for now the caravans were rolling, and money was circulating in Santa Fe. Kearny's creation of a territory of New Mexico and conferral of U.S. citizenship on the residents were both quietly disallowed by the powers in Washington, D.C., until such time as a peace treaty had been signed. But for the present, the offers were made and accepted in good faith.

The Building of Fort Marcy

On August 19, 1846, General Kearny sent lieutenants Emory and Jeremy F. Gilmer off to find a site for a fort. They selected an elevated site about 600 to 700 yards northeast of the plaza, the only point that commanded a view of the entire town.

There are number of brief descriptions of Santa Fe in 1846, none of them very flattering. A British visitor compared it to "a prairie dog town." Houses were universally built of adobe and one story high. Only the governor's palace had glass windows. In ordinary dwellings the window openings had shutters fastened on the inside with a heavy bar or else small windows closed with sheets of selenite, a translucent mineral. Room walls were whitewashed, and the smooth, earthen floors were partly covered with a locally woven black and white wool carpeting known as *jerga*. Calico tacked to the walls prevented the whitewash from rubbing off. For heating and cooking there were corner fireplaces. In addition to any furniture, room furnishings consisted of small mirrors, a few *retablos*, and perhaps a *bulto*, a carved statue of a saint. The wealthier homes had a wooden bedstead; poor families slept on the ground and rolled up their mats or blankets during the day for seats.

From their vantage point, Emory and Gilmer would have observed that Santa Fe was compact only in the vicinity of the plaza. Elsewhere the houses were interspersed among fields of corn, wheat, beans, and chile. In the neighborhood of present-day Grant Avenue and Griffin Street there were a half-dozen residences, "quite grand houses for the time." East Palace Avenue had

Jerga.

three residents, including Don Juan Sena, the owner of what is now known as Sena Plaza. The *parroquia*, the principal church in Santa Fe, stood on the present site of St. Francis Cathedral.

The center of the city was its public square or plaza, where Kearny would soon have a tall flagpole erected. An acequia, adjoined by a row of small cottonwood trees, ran along each side of the plaza. The west side was nearly all residences, near the center of which stood the post office and the store for tobacco sales, under the Mexican government's tobacco monopoly. La Castrense, the old military chapel that occupied the center of the plaza's south side, had been abandoned for some years, and part of the roof had already fallen in. On the east side about midway in the block was the *casa de cabildo*, used by the city council or *ayuntamiento* of Santa Fe. Other buildings on the east side were government offices, except for a store occupied by Don Juan Sena on the southeast corner. Sena's *tienda*, "the second best store in town" by one authority, boasted the only wooden plank floor in Santa Fe.

Elsewhere on the southeast corner there were other stores and a large residence that within a few years became a hotel, the precursor of La Fonda. On the north side, then as now, stood the long, low adobe structure known as the Palace of the Governors. The northeastern corner of the plaza had the old government storehouse, used to store merchandise brought over the Santa Fe Trail while the goods were examined by customs officials. Other buildings held shops, nearly all of them kept by American traders. Portals fronted the buildings on three sides of the plaza.

General Kearny approved his lieutenants' selection of a fort site and their plan for an earthwork enclosure or "star fort" with associated buildings. According to Lieutenant Emory, the fort was intended as a citadel to which troops could retreat "in case of extremities" and hold out until help arrived, but its chief object was the effect it would have upon the morale of the newly subjugated population of Santa Fe. Indeed, "Their own guns [i.e., the artillery captured from Armijo] will be chiefly used to garrison the fort; and with them every house in Santa Fe could be levelled on the least appearance of revolt." Hopefully this would never be necessary.

Street scene in front of the Exchange Hotel (precursor of La Fonda), 1885.

Santa Fe plaza, circa 1867.

Construction on the fort began on August 23 with a work force of one hundred soldiers, later supplemented by thirty-one Mexican brick masons. The plan of this enclosure featured ten sides, generally aligned with the sides of the hill. The embankments were built up of earth and their slopes faced with sun-dried bricks, the embrasures for the guns likewise being built of adobes. The parapets had sufficient space for mounting seventeen cannons, most of which faced towards the town. A huge ditch surrounded the whole, and the vertical distance from the bottom of the ditch to the top of the parapet was seventeen feet. General Kearny named the fortification Fort Marcy in honor of the secretary of war, William L. Marcy.

Lieutenant Gilmer directed the construction, and by early November he had the fort in a defensible state. By the end of that month the earthworks had been completed. Gilmer also started work on an arsenal, which was finished the following spring. An adobe-walled blockhouse, laid out some sixty yards from the earthworks, may have been left uncompleted. There was never any thought of housing a garrison on top of this hill, and no shot was ever fired from the fort itself.

Until 1850 the officer who commanded the Ninth Military Department (New Mexico) occupied the Palace of the Governors, and his men lived in the old Mexican barracks in the downtown area then known as the Post of Santa Fe. In time, the old Spanish and Mexican buildings were replaced, and the name Fort Marcy was transferred to the facilities at the Post of Santa Fe. The earthwork on the hill gradually went to ruin. Santa Fe retained a garrison until 1894, and two of the old Fort Marcy officers' quarters yet remain.

The Early Months of American Occupation

General Kearny established a temporary civil government in New Mexico based upon a set of laws known as the Kearny code for governing the newly acquired territory. He also appointed a set of territorial officials, including the well-known trader and Taos resident, Charles Bent, as governor, and a prominent New Mexican, Donaciano Vigil, as secretary. With everything quiet and Colonel Sterling Price due to appear at any time to garrison the territory with his Second Regiment of Missouri Mounted Volunteers, Kearny prepared to advance on California.

The general left Santa Fe on September 25 accompanied by about 300 troopers of his First Dragoons. Colonel Price arrived in the capital a week later, followed by his regiment of Missourians and five companies of volunteers known as the Mormon Battalion. Price then relieved Alexander Doniphan's men, who set off to restore peace in the Navajo country before heading south into Chihuahua. In the meantime, Kearny detached Captain Cooke from his own command to lead the Mormon Battalion on to California. By late October, Sterling Price and the officers of the new civil government were in charge of New Mexico's affairs, the Second Missouri Regiment providing most of the military force.

Even as the other columns marched away, local tensions were rising. The new volunteers lacked discipline, and there were frequent altercations between

Donaciano Vigil, territorial governor of New Mexico, 1847–48.

Ruins of Fort Marcy, circa 1915.

them and townspeople. In Santa Fe, priests and wealthy New Mexicans who saw their influence being reduced began to talk of revolt. Periodically, until Doniphan's regiment defeated and dispersed a Mexican force just north of El Paso on Christmas day, rumors flew that Mexico intended sending an army from Chihuahua to retake New Mexico. This unholy combination of rumors, disorderly conduct by the soldiers, and increasing resentment among New Mexicans led a number of leading citizens in Santa Fe and elsewhere into actively plotting the overthrow of the new government. For their part, these men considered themselves to be patriots.

Led by Tomás Ortiz, Pablo Montoya, Manuel Cortez, and the ex-colonel, Diego Archuleta, the conspirators set the evening of December 24 for a general uprising. All Americans throughout the territory and natives who had accepted positions in the territorial government were to be massacred or driven out. The wife of one conspirator leaked these plans to Colonel Price, who immediately

Diego Archuleta, 1884.

arrested a number of persons suspected of complicity and suppressed the rebellion. The two ringleaders, Ortiz and Archuleta, managed to make their escape. By early January, about the time that news of Doniphan's victory reached Santa Fe, Americans began to think that the spirit of revolt had been crushed. Governor Bent urged New Mexicans to disregard the libels spread by would-be revolutionaries and to remain quiet and support their government.

The Taos Rebellion

Two weeks after making his proclamation, Governor Bent was dead. The insurrectionists who escaped the Christmas eve roundup in Santa Fe continued to incite New Mexicans and found another opportunity when Bent and several other officials rode up to Taos in mid-January. Pablo Montoya and Tomasito, a Taos Indian leader, were already at Taos. Once they learned of the governor's presence, they enlisted anti-American Taoseños and Pueblo Indians to the cause of revolt. On the night of January 18, 1847, they roamed the streets of Taos; the following morning the insurrectionists murdered Bent and five others in the Bent home, then paraded the former governor's scalp through the town.

The same band of attackers moved a few miles north of Taos and killed seven Americans at Turley's Mill. Manuel Cortez carried news of the murders across the mountains to his home at Mora and stirred up the people there. Two Santa Fe traders happened to ride into Mora that same day and were shot as soon as they gave up their arms. Word of these murders reached the small American garrison at Las Vegas and Colonel Price in Santa Fe on January 20.

Price immediately ordered up most of the troops from Albuquerque to add to his own units, then set off to meet the rebels as soon as possible. The latter had been rousing the countryside and were advancing on Santa Fe. The American commander met them on January 24 near the town of La Cañada, now known as Santa Cruz, a few miles southeast of modern Española. He opened fire with artillery and charged the enemy's positions. Within a few minutes, he wrote, "My troops had dislodged the enemy at all points, and they were flying in every direction." He continued in the direction of Taos, and by January 28 his ranks had swelled to almost 480 regulars and volunteers. The following day they met the rebels again in the pass at Embudo. After a stiff fight, Price drove the enemy away and resumed marching on Taos.

At Taos Pueblo, the insurrectionists had fortified themselves in the church. Colonel Price's artillery finally breached the church walls, and his men stormed the rebel position. This broke the back of the defense, and the remaining insurrectionists fled or laid down their arms. The battle ended near nightfall on February 4 with some 150 of the enemy and 7 soldiers killed. The prisoners were held for trial; later that spring six of them, including Pablo Montoya, were hanged for their crimes.

The other principal action took place at the village of Mora. Hearing that the murderers had remained there after killing the traders, Captain Israel Hendley collected eighty soldiers at Las Vegas and started for Mora. They found the insurgents, and a pitched battle followed. After three hours of fighting, Hendley was shot down, and his lieutenants called off the attack. On February 1 some 200 of the Missouri volunteers returned and torched every building in Mora, destroying foodstuffs and everything else that would burn.

The Taos rebellion was the last organized revolt against American authority in New Mexico. Isolated raids and skirmishing continued through 1847; one of the raiders, Manuel Cortez, was found to have a captain's commission in the Mexican army. Partisan attacks on Price's grazing camps and retribution by the soldiers led to substantial casualties on both sides, including six inhabitants from one small village who were hanged after their conviction by a military court.

The signing of a peace treaty in February 1848 brought the war between the United States and Mexico to a close. New Mexico was now indisputably a part of the United States. Guerilla raids and threats by insurrectionists faded away, leaving the army and civilians free to face the centuries-old problem posed by the hostile Indians, particularly the Navajos, who surrounded the territory. It would be almost forty years before General Kearny's prophecy that his government would "correct all this" could be fulfilled.

Charles Bent, first territorial governor of New Mexico.

Arrival of a caravan at Santa Fe.

Santa Fe in the Days of the Trail

MARC SIMMONS

If any single event of the nineteenth century can be said to have shaped the character and determined the future of New Mexico's capital city, surely it would have to be the opening of the Santa Fe Trail in 1821. When an uneducated Missouri adventurer named William Becknell reached the plaza on November 16 of that year with a handful of companions and a string of pack mules loaded with trade goods, he had no way of knowing that his epic-making trip had launched a spectacular chapter in Southwestern history, one that would ultimately transform the lives of Santa Fe's citizenry.

At that date, the capital, population 5,000, was an unlovely huddle of one-story adobe buildings grouped around a plaza, a weathered governor's palace, and several chocolate-brown churches whose numerous bells daily created a din, according to one traveler, that could wake the dead. On the bare and dusty plaza, devoid of any hint of greenery, rose a single pole from which fluttered the flag of the new nation of Mexico. It had been the consummation of independence from Spain, in September of 1821, that allowed Missourian Becknell to enter the city freely and subsequently dispose of his wares at a large profit.

Under the Spanish colonial regime, commerce between the outlying province of New Mexico and foreign merchants from the United States had been strictly prohibited. The tight monopolistic policy of the king obliged New Mexicans to purchase all their manufactured goods at Chihuahua City, or points south, so that sales and profits could accrue to the benefit of the empire. The result was that many people on the frontier had to do without, so great was the cost of transportation and the markups of innumerable middle men.

Young Lieutenant Zebulon Pike, who had strayed into Spanish territory back in 1807 and was briefly held a prisoner in Santa Fe, saw the shining commercial possibilities that awaited American businessmen should the barriers to trade ever be dismantled. When they were, following directly upon the break with Spain, Santa Fe and neighboring towns north and south entered a new and quite unaccustomed era of prosperity.

In giving William Becknell a courteous welcome, Governor Facundo Melgares signaled the change in attitude and the beginning of a laissez-faire policy that would make possible the rapid rise of the lucrative Santa Fe trade. Americans, heretofore excluded from New Mexico, would now be at liberty to import merchandise and conduct business and even to settle permanently, said the governor. That was the word Becknell carried home to the Missouri border, and when it spread, many townsmen and farmers who had never thought of themselves as merchants decided to try their hand in the new overland trade with Santa Fe.

A Thoroughfare of Commerce

In the years that followed, the trail to New Mexico became a major international thoroughfare of commerce and a funnel by which not only foreign goods but foreign ideas, habits, and tastes were introduced to the isolated peoples of the Southwest. The American trader, questing for profits, scarcely perceived that his business ventures were fueling the beginnings of a cultural transformation among the Spanish-speaking New Mexicans. For him, Santa Fe had taken on the aspect of an exotic Eden—one where a man could go, indulge his hunger for novel experiences in a place whose customs were utterly strange, and, if he was lucky and the markets were brisk, make a small fortune in the bargain. That simple motivation drove him to risk the ever dangerous crossing of the prairies. The long-range effects of his activity upon New Mexico and the New Mexicans was probably something he never even considered.

In 1824 the first large freight caravan reached Santa Fe, consisting of twenty-three wagons and a small cannon, with eighty-one men. A member of

Lieutenant Zebulon Pike.

the party, Augustus Storrs—postmaster of Franklin, Missouri, turned trader—records that the value of their goods upon purchase at home was $35,000. When his stock was sold or traded at Santa Fe it returned $180,000, mostly in Spanish milled dollars but including some gold and silver bullion, beaver pelts, and mules. Storrs, who would soon be named the first U.S. consul for Santa Fe, also informs us that the American merchandise was made up of cotton and woolen items, light articles of cutlery, silk shawls, looking glasses, and "many other articles necessary for the purposes of an assortment." Afterward, we know that such things as books, paper, pens, religious medals, and colored prints of the saints formed a part of every merchants "assortment."

To a greater or lesser degree all imports had an impact upon cultural life as well as the provincial economy. An example can be found in the small printing press with its fonts of type, the first ever seen in New Mexico, which was carried to Santa Fe by famed merchant Josiah Gregg in 1834. It was probably a special order, placed by a prominent citizen of the capital, Ramón Abreu. At least he was soon listed as publisher of Santa Fe's first newspaper, *El Crepúsculo de la Libertad* (the dawn of liberty), which attracted fifty subscribers but folded after four issues. Ramón Abreu fared no better, dying in the short but bloody revolution that engulfed Santa Fe three years later. His little press ended up in a room of the governor's palace, where it was occasionally used to print handbills and dodgers. Then it fell into the hands of Padre Antonio José Martínez, who moved it to Taos.

Observant travelers who came over the Santa Fe Trail and were moved by the beauty of the city's natural setting and the novelty of the architecture and local custom often set down detailed descriptions of what they saw. One such early-day writer was Matt Field, a Santa Fe visitor in 1839 and later an assistant editor of the New Orleans *Picayune*, which published serially his articles on New Mexico. Field thought Santa Fe's adobe residences resembled "an assemblage of mole hills," and he noted that buildings were all one story, simply because land was cheap and the practical inhabitants preferred rooms six to a row rather than apartments piled on one another since it was easier to go through a doorway than climb a flight of stairs.

Instituciones De Derecho De Castilla Y De Indies by José María Álvarez. Published by Padre Antonio José Martinez, printed by Jesus María Baca, in Taos, New Mexico, in 1842 on the first printing press to be brought to New Mexico.

East San Francisco Street at the plaza, 1868–69.

The situation with regard to two-stories, however, was soon to change, particularly on the plaza, as the pressure grew from American merchants to acquire summer store space in this central location. The eastern side of the plaza was taken up by the Mexican customs house and associated storerooms (where the Catron Building is today), and next to that the *ayuntamiento*, or municipal offices. Opposite, on the west side stood the post office, and on the south in the center of the block was the Castrense, or military chapel. In between, other structures were mostly private homes whose owners profited from the booming overland trade by seasonally renting their front rooms to foreign store keepers. Even Governor Manuel Armijo, himself heavily invested in the commerce with Missouri, was not above renting out rooms in the palace when demand was especially heavy.

By the 1830s it was the habit of the Missouri merchants to leave Independence or Westport (now part of Kansas City) in the spring so as to arrive in Santa Fe by early summer. At the customs house on the plaza they paid the required duties on their freight, and then many of them scurried to rent a store and commence retailing. Others sold at wholesale to local businessmen or those from neighboring towns or Mexico. In any case the aim was to sell out as quickly as possible and return home with the profits before the first snowfall swept across the plains.

The Chihuahua Trade

It was not long, however, before a serious trade imbalance appeared. The flow of goods from the States was so large in volume that little Santa Fe could not conveniently absorb it all. Some of the Americans, finding themselves stuck with surpluses, tried spending the winter in hopes that a trickle of sales during the off season would finally deplete their stock. But many others attempted a different course: from Santa Fe they directed their freight wagons down the old Camino Real to Chihuahua City, which had a population twice as large and was also rich, owing to nearby silver mines. For the more daring and enterprising, Santa Fe thus became a mere way station on the long trail to the Chihuahua market.

That Santa Fe did not entirely lose its place as a vital trade center can be attributed mainly to the entry of the New Mexican merchant class into this far-flung commerce. Members of the Pino, Ortiz, Delgado, Otero, Chávez, and other patrician families decided not to be left on the sidelines. They organized their own wagon trains and went east on the trail to buy directly from wholesalers. Returning with their freight to the Santa Fe customs house, they paid duties at a rate substantially lower than that imposed upon Americans. This favoritism, shown Mexican merchants, allowed them to undersell their foreign competitors and prosper.

The New Mexicans further enlarged their success by intensifying the trade with Chihuahua that had existed since colonial times. Santa Fe under Spanish rule had stagnated as a small and isolated market at the terminus of the Camino Real. But now, with the opening of the trail from the United States,

Aristocratic New Mexico don.

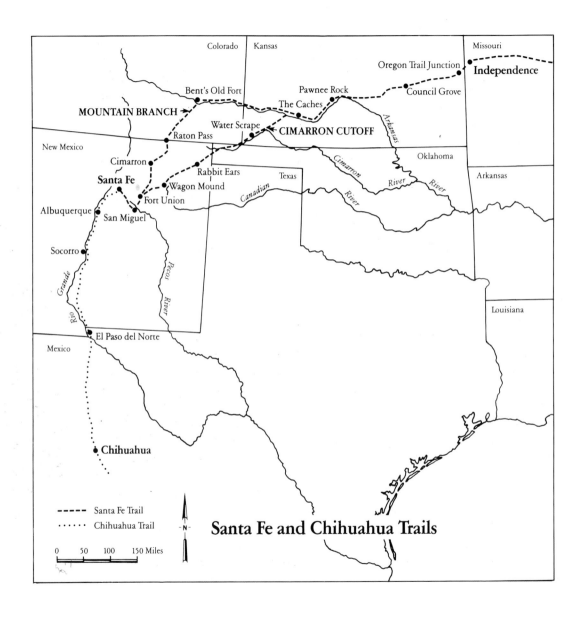

Colorado   Kansas   Missouri

Oregon Trail Junction   **Independence**

Bent's Old Fort   Pawnee Rock

Council Grove

The Caches

MOUNTAIN BRANCH →

Water Scrape   **CIMARRON CUTOFF**

Raton Pass

New Mexico   Oklahoma

Cimarron

Rabbit Ears   Texas   Arkansas

Santa Fe

Wagon Mound

Fort Union

Albuquerque

San Miguel

Socorro

Louisiana

El Paso del Norte

Mexico

Chihuahua

Arkansas

Cimarron River

Canadian

Pecos River

Rio Grande

- - - - Santa Fe Trail
· · · · Chihuahua Trail

Santa Fe and Chihuahua Trails

0   50   100   150 Miles

-N-

New Mexico's capital suddenly found itself in the center rather than at the end of the flow of overland traffic. The native merchants of Santa Fe, thereby, were well positioned to become middlemen and, in so doing, build personal fortunes. By 1843, according to several contemporary sources, New Mexicans outnumbered American travelers on the Santa Fe Trail, and that, added to the brisk Chihuahua trade, meant that the provincial economy had begun a recovery from the earlier imbalances.

In 1846 Private John T. Hughes, a member of the invading United States Army, was able to describe Santa Fe as "the great emporium where the merchants of central Mexico annually met the American caravans, to purchase their stocks. It is a city of considerable trade." Just how considerable is suggested by some figures available for that year. Caravans reaching Santa Fe had a total of 636 wagons, engaging 750 teamsters and drovers, and carrying $1 million worth of goods. While true that a significant portion of the freight continued on to Chihuahua and other interior cities, the import duties collected in Santa Fe and the stimulation of local business as a result of the booming international commerce directly benefited New Mexicans.

Josiah Gregg.

The dramatic aspect of this activity, particularly that associated with the arrival of a caravan from the plains, is best depicted by trader Josiah Gregg in his classic book, *Commerce of the Prairies*, first published in 1844. Approaching the limits of Santa Fe, the merchants and teamsters engaged in "clamorous rejoicings." And Gregg adds, "Even the animals seemed to participate in the humor of their riders, who grew more and more merry and obstreperous as they descended towards the city. I doubt, in short, whether the first sight of the walls of Jerusalem were beheld by the crusaders with much more tumultuous and soul-enrapturing joy."

As the huge wagons rumbled slowly down the last half mile of the Santa Fe Trail to the plaza, the air was filled with sharp pops, not unlike bursts of Fourth of July firecrackers. For the occasion, the wagoners had tied brand new "poppers" to the end of their whips, and they vied with one another to make the most noise. Crowds lined the dusty thoroughfare and added to the bustle and excitement by shouting, *"Los Americanos! Los carros! La entrada de la*

The Elsberg-Amberg wagon train in Santa Fe's plaza, October 1861. This is the oldest known photograph of the plaza.

caravana!" In short, it was a spectacle that now belongs to history and can never be repeated.

Part of the allure of Santa Fe for the first generation of American newcomers lay in the fact that it was a foreign capital. Most of the men from Missouri had never ventured outside of their own country, and the prospect of a trip to New Mexico—with its different language, strange customs, and distinctive architecture—held all the trappings of a romantic adventure. It offered the chance to escape from the humdrum at home and perhaps get wealthy in the bargain.

American Conquest and Its Impact

That side of the trail experience, however, was irrevocably altered by the turbulent events of 1846. With the outbreak of the Mexican War, Colonel (later General) Stephen W. Kearny marched over the trail and on August 18 unfurled the Stars and Stripes from the rooftop of the governor's palace. All at once the Santa Fe Trail was no longer the international road that it had been since 1821. Now both ends of the trail were in the hands of the United States, and while the atmosphere of Santa Fe remained foreign, its politics and economy began to move in directions familiar to Americans.

One of the most visible signs of change was the presence of English-speaking soldiers throughout the city, there to keep order but also to protect the citizenry from Navajos and Apaches who occasionally raided on the outskirts of Santa Fe. They were attached to Fort Marcy, an earthworks begun by General Kearny and located on a hill northeast of the plaza. About them, Susan Magoffin, wife of veteran trader Samuel Magoffin, wrote, "What an everlasting noise these soldiers keep up—from early dawn till late at night they are blowing their trumpets, whooping like Indians, or making some unheard of sounds, quite shocking to my delicate nerves."

Many of the troops who garrisoned Santa Fe over the next two years were short-term enlistees who had signed up during the heated excitement at the beginning of the Mexican War. When their enlistments were up, the majority of them returned to Missouri over the Santa Fe Trail, but some decided they liked the easy, colorful ways of the capital and remained. Several of them founded the first American newspaper in New Mexico, the *Santa Fe Republican*, which was printed in both English and Spanish. The initial issue appeared in September 1847 and came from a press the army had freighted over the trail from St. Louis earlier that year. On May 13, 1848, the paper gave a graphic account of changes that had overtaken Santa Fe in the two years since the Kearny conquest.

One of those changes made a strong impression on young Francisco Chávez after his return to Santa Fe following several years' schooling in Missouri. "Money was now more plentifully distributed in and about Santa Fe,

A banquet at Headquarters Building, Fort Marcy, circa 1890.

than at any other time in its long history," he declared. "Every man that wished to be employed had some sort of occupation, for which he was being regularly paid." The reason, he observed, was that the paymaster regularly brought the army payroll under escort from Fort Leavenworth, not only to pay the troops but also to furnish the sums for purchase of foodstores, hay and grain, mules, construction supplies, and labor. The influx of outside cash stimulated local business as much as the continued expansion of civilian commercial traffic.

Another innovation in Santa Fe life that soon made its appearance was regular mail service. In former days mail had come up the Camino Real from Mexico once a month, if the Apaches did not interfere. After the American occupation, military couriers and private travelers on the Santa Fe Trail carried mail from the States in a rather haphazard fashion until 1850, when the first government contracts were let to transport the mail on a regular basis. On one of the inaugural runs, the post wagon, bearing eleven riders, was attacked and burned by Utes and Jicarilla Apaches at Wagon Mound, in eastern New Mexico. The men all died, but a military patrol was able to recover much of the mail that lay scattered across the plain.

David Waldo of Independence, the initial mail contractor, was also a chief investor in the first stage line to link Missouri with New Mexico. In the Spanish and Mexican periods, Santa Fe had not enjoyed the blessings of stagecoach service to anywhere. So, when a monthly run from Independence began on July 1, 1850, it was a sign that New Mexico's capital had taken another step toward casting off the bonds imposed by isolation and provincialism. In 1857 the service was upgraded to twice a month, and a new contracting company, Hockaday and Hall, announced in the Santa Fe press that their coaches were "entirely new and comfortable for passengers. Travelers to and from New Mexico will doubtless find this the safest . . . and cheapest mode of crossing the plains. Provisions, arms and ammunition furnished by the proprietors."

During the last thirty years the Santa Fe Trail was in existence, the volume and value of goods shipped increased enormously. Much of this was in the form of military freight destined for new forts that sprang to life along the trail, but the Santa Fe and New Mexico markets also absorbed their share owing to

The "Mountain Pride" stagecoach on display at the Palace of the Governors Museum.

"Santa Fe Plaza in the 1880s," painting by Francis X. Grosshenney.

The American influence on Santa Fe's architectural style is apparent in this 1880s picture of Fort Marcy officers' quarters along Lincoln Avenue.

the rise in purchasing power that accompanied economic growth in the new territory. Some idea of the magnitude of the activity in these later decades can be gathered from figures recorded for 1860: engaged in the overland trade that year were 5,948 men, 2,170 wagons, and 17,836 oxen. Each wagon bore on the average 5,500 pounds of freight. The total value of transported goods for the year was estimated at $3,500,000.

The impact of this vigorous enterprise upon Santa Fe's society and traditional culture was necessarily profound. Those Hispanic residents of the mercantile class who profited from the new economic and political order adapted quickly to American fashions in dress, foods, household furnishings, and even architectural styles. Changes affecting the poorer classes were less pervasive. Among them the older customs and original patterns of domestic life persisted alongside the foreign introductions that symbolized the dawn of a new era. As a result, Joseph P. Allyn, upon completing a journey over the trail in 1863, could see the town with the fresh eyes of a newcomer and proclaim, "Santa Fe is a strange chapter torn out of the past and stuck in between the leaves of American progress."

Another observer of this period, Marian Sloan Russell, first saw Santa Fe as a child of seven in 1852, having come with her mother in a caravan led by the celebrated wagonmaster Francis X. Aubry. Approaching the eastern outskirts as Josiah Gregg had done a generation before, she exclaimed, "How our hearts waited for a sight of the Santa Fe of our dreams. We thought it would be a city and waited breathlessly for the first sight of towers and tall turrets. We crossed a water ditch . . . then passed through a great wooden gateway that arched high above us. We were in Santa Fe."

Marian made other trips on the trail, and despite her close familiarity with Santa Fe, the dove-colored adobe town never lost its image as a place filled with romance and adventure. She even had her first meeting alone with her future husband, Lieutenant Richard Russell, under the tall welcoming arch that spanned the trail somewhere east of the plaza. Only Marian, among thousands of travelers, mentions the presence of that arch. But many others succumbed to the charms of an old-world Santa Fe, just as she did.

By 1870, when the advancing railroad reached southeastern Colorado, it was clear that the days of the Santa Fe Trail were numbered. Early in 1879 the tracks of the AT & SF descended from Raton Pass onto the plains of New Mexico, and by the Fourth of July they were in Las Vegas. The trail, thereby, was reduced to a mere sixty-five miles, from the railhead to Santa Fe. One stage line, Barlow, Sanderson & Co., and one freighting outfit remained in operation throughout the remainder of the year and into January of the next.

Finally, on February 9, 1880, the first engine steamed into Santa Fe on a spur from the main line, which had bypassed the capital eighteen miles to the southeast. The *Weekly New Mexican* that day hailed the red-letter event with these bold headlines:

"Baby" on Glorieta summit, October 1880.

SANTA FE'S TRIUMPH!
THE LAST LINK IS FORGED IN THE
IRON CHAIN WHICH BINDS THE
ANCIENT CITY TO THE
UNITED STATES

And The Old Santa Fe Trail
Passes Into Oblivion

It was perhaps a fitting epitaph for the sixty-year-old trail. The flow of traffic during its long life had brought with it new people, new goods, new ideas, all serving to transform Santa Fe and connect it, however tenuously, to events in a far and alien world. The trail, as a forerunner of the railroad, helped prepare the way for the inevitable changes that would accompany the westward march of technology. But in the end, the Santa Fe Trail was to be remembered best for a rich and lively history, which after all may be its most enduring legacy.

The Palace of the Governors

CARRIE FORMAN ARNOLD

The Palace of the Governors in Santa Fe is probably the oldest public building in the United States. Still useful as a museum of the Southwest and exhibition hall, it is the city's centerpiece. The portal of the palace, overlooking the plaza, daily shelters a lively mix of Pueblo Indians and visitors.

The palace has been known by several names during the last 370-odd years. At the turn of the twentieth century, when interest in Spanish history began to overcome Anglo distaste for "mud" construction, writers increasingly began using the term *el palacio* instead of *adobe palace*. After the building became a museum, the name was formalized to today's *Palace of the Governors*. For several hundred years in the Spanish records, it was most often referred to as the *casas reales* (royal houses) or *palacio real* (royal palace). Indeed, the *palacio real* may have been quite royal for its day on the far frontier.

Beginnings: 1609–1680

Under King Philip III of Spain, Don Pedro de Peralta was appointed governor and captain general of the province of Nuevo Mexico in 1609. He engineered the design of the capital city on a sheltered bank of the Santa Fe River. Under Peralta's direction during the winter of 1609–10, the seat of government was moved from San Gabriel (near present-day Española) to Santa Fe.

Peralta had to bring in supplies, animals, and staff from Zacatecas, Mexico. Since the supply caravan did not leave until the fall of 1609, little if any construction was probably accomplished that year. But a fortified shelter must have been a priority as soon as any major construction began.

Opposite page: The Palace of the Governors, 1868.

Chess pieces (above) and majolica
bowl (below) found in excavations
at the Palace of the Governors.

During those first difficult and fearful years, rough buildings of simple construction probably provided immediate shelter. Spanish regulations decreed that the design of frontier settlements should be "defensive," particularly because the local Indians had few reasons to love the Spanish strangers.

Archaeological examination of the southeast room of the palace has shown evidence of ancient walls. Some were *jacal*, a palisade of upright timbers set into a trench with mud caulking for solidity. Buildings of this type still exist in New Mexico. The old walls may have been roofed for living spaces or left open to the sky as corrals for the stock. There is also evidence of old adobe walls at the palace. In any case, between 1609 and 1680, a palatial building did arise on the north side of the plaza, built at least in part of massive adobe walls.

The *casas reales* in Santa Fe probably seemed impossibly distant to the royal Court of Madrid. Still, Nuevo Mexico was the property of the Spanish Crown. The governors of New Mexico were the king's direct representatives via the viceroy of Mexico. Thus, the royal houses of Santa Fe reflected the prestige and power of the king of Spain. The governor's home enhanced his noble position and served the needs of administration and defense. Indeed, although many records were destroyed in the Pueblo Revolt of 1680, there are hints that in the seventeenth century the palace was quite an impressive structure, considering its remoteness on the New Mexico frontier.

Around 1657, the governor, Don Bernardo López de Mendizábal, and his lady, Doña Teresa, ran afoul of the Inquisition. In those days, the expense of the suspect's jail stay was met by the sale of his or her property. Lists of the governor's possessions made when the couple was carted off to Mexico City under arrest and the trial records provide an intriguing glimpse of life within the *casas reales* of Santa Fe.

Governor López de Mendizábal had several figures of Christ. "One of these was on a altar in his wife's drawing room, under a canopy so high that a ladder was required to reach up to clean it. The other statue was under a canopy at the head of his bed, where it was more accessible." In a peculiar room arrangement, there was a room of horse equipment between Doña Teresa's dressing room and the office of the secretary. Among their possessions were writing desks, books, silver tableware, rich clothes, and a private carriage.

Inhabitants of the adobe palace of the seventeenth century certainly enjoyed some luxuries. An idea of the quality of life at the palace before 1680 may be found below the level of today's floor in the west end of the palace. Archaeological excavations uncovered remains of a floor of adobe bricks beautifully laid in a diagonal pattern. They also yielded parts of a finely carved chess set dating from before the revolt. Pieces of Chinese porcelain are also likely to date from the same time.

Scholars have differing points of view concerning the location of the *casas reales* in the seventeenth century. Traditional theory holds that these public buildings formed a square compound extending into the property north of the back wall of the present Palace of the Governors. Until the middle of the nineteenth century, the front of the building was approximately 350 feet long. If square, the structure would have extended to the south edge of the First Interstate Bank Building. The present museum administration building at 113 Lincoln Avenue would have been well inside the interior patio. Workrooms, stables, and storage rooms are likely to have been located along the back wall and sides. Perhaps soldiers were garrisoned there too. If so, the central enclosed patio was probably more than four times the size of the palace patio today. At the southeast corner, the palace had a massive tower containing a chapel with at least one exterior door. Other towers also may have existed.

A typical *zaguan* (a double-doored entrance wide enough for a wagon to pass through) opened from the center of the palace off the main plaza into the huge interior patio. Metal grates were available and may have protected some windows. By 1650, the main entrance featured a pair of small cannon.

An alternate theory concerning the early location of the palace, proposed by Cordelia Thomas Snow, has it surrounding the plaza to the south. This rectangular plaza, probably 731 feet in length by 480 feet across, was much larger than the plaza of today and would have extended from its present western boundary east to St. Francis Cathedral and from the present Palace of the Governors south almost to Water Street.

Typical Santa Fe *zaguan,* or covered entrance way.

Since no copy of the complete plan of seventeenth-century Santa Fe is known to exist, and since downtown construction activity has disturbed archaeological remains, there is insufficient evidence to prove either theory.

Revolt and Change: 1680–1692

At any period in the history of the palace, one can find references to rebuilding or repair. Its walls, like those of all adobe structures, could be remarkably durable if protected and maintained. In the spring of 1680, Governor Otermín found the palace compound "in ruins and falling down, with many gates open and without even doors at the principal entrances." He spent several months supervising the repair and fortification of the *casas reales,* and his repairs proved timely. Beyond the walls of his palace, several years of drought and poor crops had aggravated existing conflicts with the Pueblo Indians. In August 1680, these grievances fueled the bloody Pueblo Revolt. Otermín later wrote that the repairs were finished only eight days before the revolt erupted.

The size of the structure during the siege is indicated in Otermín's papers, in which he mentions that about a thousand Spaniards and their servants gathered in the *casas reales.* In addition, it sheltered 5,000 sheep and goats, 430 horses and mules, and 300 head of cattle, all without crowding.

After the Spaniards abandoned the city, the Indians destroyed much that they felt showed evil Spanish influence. In the process, they remodeled the *casas reales* into a large pueblo. Visible today, a thick center wall runs most of the length of the palace. During the revolt, the roof over rooms to the north of this wall, in the west part of the palace, was destroyed. In the 1970s, archaeologists uncovered deep storage pits under a floor north of the center wall. Discovered in an area that seems to have been an outdoor area when they were constructed, the pits were usually bell shaped and up to six feet deep. Some had been plastered inside. The pits are now thought to have been built by the occupying Indians for storing foods such as dried grains.

Ceramic bowl excavated from under the palace.

Above, archaeological excavations at the palace in mid-1970s. *Below:* projectile points found under the palace.

Rooms to the south of the great center wall on today's plaza side of the building also offered revelations to the archaeologists. There is evidence that during the Indian occupation, many rooms—including the one with the fine brick floor—were divided into typical, small, pueblo-style rooms. Doors and presumably windows were filled in with adobe. Ladders leading down from roof openings were used for access. Evidence of fires in pueblo-style fireplaces was also found.

Another fascinating feature found by the archaeologists may be evidence of a rudimentary running water system, apparently built while the Indians occupied the palace. A mysterious little trench, discovered leading from the protected inner plaza into the Indians' living quarters, seems to have been lined with wood and fine sand. Although the purpose of this feature is not entirely clear, Don Diego de Vargas mentioned water conduits leading into the building in his reports to the king after the Reconquest of 1692–93.

Acequias flowed from high on the Santa Fe River northwest into Santa Fe; with the help of a few springs in the *ciénega* (swamp) northeast of the palace, they provided water for the people and their gardens. One acequia flowed in front of the palace as late as the American period (after 1846). Another flowed through the area generally covered by Marcy Street today. A plan of the palace property drawn by the Historic American Buildings Survey during the 1930s shows buried evidence of an acequia in the palace patio, approximately where the walkway in front of the Press of the Palace of the Governors is today. Various trenches in streets and driveways near the palace have shown evidence of old acequias in the area, running generally east to west. Small trenches could have brought water directly into the building from one of these acequias to the north.

One thing is clear from the archaeological investigations: in the seventeenth century, the *casas reales* did not look at all like the building that we see today. While the great center wall seems to have been built by 1680, many earlier walls do not align with later walls at all. Sadly, so little remains of pre-revolt walls, especially outside the existing building, and so few records seem to have been saved, that the appearance of the earliest *casas reales* may never be known.

Reconquest and Reconstruction: 1692–1789

In 1692, Don Diego de Vargas, leading a military expedition from El Paso, arrived at Santa Fe on the morning of September 13. He later described an amazing sight: the former *casas reales* had been turned into a multistoried Indian pueblo occupied by members of the Tewa and Tano tribes. Ruins of Spanish dwellings had been connected to form a walled fortress enclosing two large plazas. Archaeology and the historical shape of the city suggest that the *casas reales* became the base of a multistoried structure.

Historians differ about the shape and arrangement of the early plazas of Santa Fe, and the historical and archaeological references are vague. It seems quite possible that the palace separated the two plazas. If so, the south plaza

Opposite page, modern-day aerial view of downtown Santa Fe showing probable extent of the palace and presidio in the late eighteenth century.

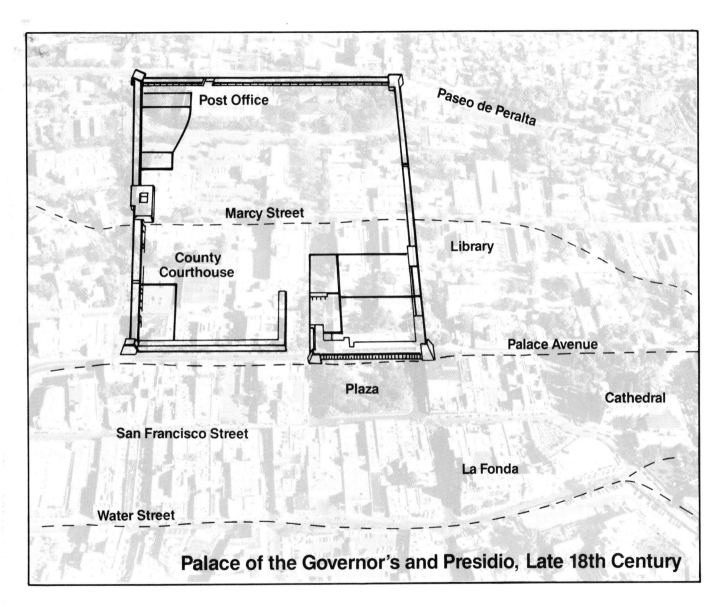

Palace of the Governor's and Presidio, Late 18th Century

Post Office

Paseo de Peralta

Marcy Street

Library

County
Courthouse

Palace Avenue

Plaza

Cathedral

San Francisco Street

La Fonda

Water Street

Portal of the Palace of the Governors.

would correspond generally with the one that exists today. The north plaza was probably the patio of the Spanish *casas reales,* where the refugees' animals had been gathered and later where the Indians dug storage pits. This pueblo fortress was further protected by towers at its corners. Providing the only access, a door in the center of the south wall, facing the river, could be defended from a fortification above. A walled passage to limit access and provide cover for defending the structure led to the door. It must have been an awe-inspiring structure.

During this mostly symbolic visit, the Spaniards had their first look at the changes that the Indians had made in the city. Some time later, after Vargas and a group of colonists had actually reoccupied it, he described the walled pueblo to the king. "There were so many living quarters, including those that had been built over the palacio, that it took a whole day to take a complete inventory." At least some of Vargas's account has been corroborated by other evidence, such as the archaeological discovery of early Spanish rooms divided into pueblo-style cubicles and reached by ladders through the ceilings.

Governor Vargas favored a defendable fortress, but the colonists evidently preferred separate home sites. Vargas went to jail (not necessarily because of that issue), and while he was incarcerated, the Indian fortress was dismantled. Sometime after the Reconquest, the Indian storage pits were filled with trash and debris, and rooms were built again on top of them in the inner plaza. Once again, the shape of the *casas reales* had been drastically changed.

In the eighteenth century, the aging building needed frequent repairs. How much was only repair and how much was new construction is difficult to determine from the records. Tree-ring dates from some of the vigas in the palace range from 1711 throughout the eighteenth century. Governor Marqués de la Peñuela even petitioned the Crown for permission to demolish the building in 1708. He apparently gave up, and eight years later Governor Don Felix Martínez reported that the *casas reales* were barely standing—and then only with the aid of many buttresses and timber props. Several south entrances were mentioned. One led through the governor's quarters into a patio, probably a walled-off segment of the large, old north plaza. Another entrance, a typical *zaguan,* opened to another patio. It is difficult to tell how many courtyards were behind the building at that time. One had a stable with a small, two-wheeled carriage and a dry well with a wooden bucket. Two towers, one of which contained gunpowder, were in particularly miserable condition.

While properly maintained adobe can be remarkably durable, lack of constant maintenance can quickly weaken a structure. In addition, the archaeological investigations revealed that the fill in the storage pits and other holes evidently was not allowed to settle before the impatient Spaniards rebuilt walls, causing them to slump. Numerous postholes uncovered in the areas of investigation indicate that the building was indeed propped up in rooms dating to the Reconquest.

Lieutenant Governor Pedro de Villasur probably saw the building in this condition as he led an ill-fated expedition against the French and Pawnees in June 1720. The Spaniards, wearing broad-brimmed hats, and their Pueblo Indian allies, wearing their long hair tied behind, rode off to meet the enemy. The disastrous battle that ensued in present-day Nebraska was depicted by an unknown artist on tanned hides. This remarkable painting, now known as one of the Segesser paintings, is proudly displayed today in the Palace of the Governors.

When Bishop Tamarón stayed in the *casas reales* in 1760, he noted that it had no fortress. In fact, the entire town was so spread out along the river that defense would have been difficult. Governor Juan Bautista de Anza, an able soldier and diplomat, decided that a new fortress and government building should be constructed in Barrio de Analco, on the higher south side of the river. During his term as governor (1777–89), he planned to destroy the palace, abandon the plaza, and rebuild in the barrio in a more compact and defendable manner. Some of the citizens were so incensed by the idea that they covertly left town and took their complaint to a higher authority in Mexico. In Arizpe, the commandant general agreed to block the move, and Anza gave up.

About the same time, King Charles III wanted some elk for his royal zoo in Madrid. Governor Anza managed to capture eight New Mexican elk, and while he awaited further orders, the elk apparently were corralled behind the

The death of Pedro de Villasur as depicted in the Segesser hide painting.

palace. Communication with Spain was slow, and the royal elk were less than ideal guests. They attacked people and had such large appetites that the governor was forced to tap an emergency military fund to feed them. Finally, orders arrived, and the elk were sent by caravan to Mexico City. Governor Anza was then ordered to capture a new herd of elk in the event that misfortune should befall the first bunch. Historian Marc Simmons has speculated that Governor Anza enjoyed a royal elk dinner in the palace when word came that some of the original animals had finally arrived safely at the Court of Madrid so that the others would not be needed.

Frontier Presidio: 1789–1821

Perhaps Governor Anza's concern about defense also traveled back to the king, who ordered a study of the frontier posts. A group of royal engineers was sent into New Mexico, directed by the Marqués de Rubí. In 1766, a member of the corps, Joseph de Urrutia, prepared a detailed map of Santa Fe. The document contains the earliest known mapped image of the palace and clearly records its relationship to other buildings in the city at that time.

The map shows a long building fronting the plaza and featuring slight projections at each end—perhaps towers or bastions. The depth of the building was fairly uniform except for the western third, where the palace may have had a sheltered passageway, and the building narrowed to the north. The indented passage may have indicated a *zaguan* or gate through the building into the north patio. Gardens were shown beyond the north patio. Other buildings in the town clustered along San Francisco Street, bordered the plaza, or were scattered along the Santa Fe River.

Probably in response to the Rubí reports, and concerned about territorial claims of other foreign powers in the New World, Spain determined to strengthen frontier defenses. In Santa Fe, the palace was to become the cornerstone of a mammoth new fortress—the presidio. Despite terrible rain storms that melted many of the adobes intended for its construction, it was started in 1789 and completed in 1791.

A plan of the Santa Fe presidio, drawn in Chihuahua from descriptions by people familiar with the structure, shows that in the new fortress, the old palace formed the extreme southeast corner of a huge quadrangle. A great wall extended north from the corner of today's Palace Avenue and Washington Street all the way to the front of the Scottish Rite Temple at Paseo de Peralta. There the wall turned west to enclose the site of today's post office complex, then south along the present site of Grant Street, then east toward the palace, on what is now Palace Avenue, in front of the current location of the Museum of Fine Arts.

The Palace of the Governors, 1880s.

The presidio had towers on the corners. In the middle of the south side of the presidio, just east of today's Museum of Fine Arts, a large entrance allowed access to the open fields within the structure. In times of danger, the garrison horses could be corralled there for easy availability. A jail occupied the west end of the palace next to this entrance. Soldiers' quarters built all around the inside of the quadrangle walls seem to have been in neglected condition in 1807, when they were duly noted by a young American, Lieutenant Zebulon M. Pike, when he arrived in Santa Fe as a prisoner. His report was the first American eyewitness account of Santa Fe. Before he and his men were sent on to Chihuahua, Pike dined with Governor Joaquin de Real Alencaster in the palace. He described the dinner as "rather splendid." They were served "wines of the Southern Provinces," wrote Pike, "and when His Excellency was a little warmed with the influence of the cheering liquor, he became very sociable, and expressed his opinion freely."

Mexican Transition: 1821–1846

The celebration of Mexican independence was led in January 1821 by Governor Facundo Melgares. As a young soldier, he had escorted Pike and the American soldiers as prisoners. Now, however, Americans were welcomed and even took part in the festivities, which culminated in a *baile* (ball) in the palace.

Mexico had too many financial problems at home to incur expenses on distant frontiers, and from 1821 to 1846 the fortunes of the palace depended upon the finances of its governors. Some of them did very well as a result of duties placed on trade goods arriving over the Santa Fe Trail from the United States. Before he was beheaded by a mob in 1837, Governor Pérez brought large gilded mirrors, a big table clock, and sofas upholstered in calico to the palace.

The walled presidio and the palace were again neglected, but occasionally, the governors spent money on renovations. Expensive glass windows were installed before 1832. Archaeological studies suggest that in the nineteenth century, more of the floors were carefully prepared with a layer of fine adobe over adobe brick than they had been.

A small acequia ran in front of the main doorway, which was evidently large enough for a mounted rider to enter. One of the governors, General Mariano Martínez de Lejanza, planted cottonwood trees in the plaza. These were watered by an acequia. Shortly after dawn one morning in 1844, a party of disgruntled Ute Indians attacked Governor Martínez in his palace office. While he held the attackers off with a chair, his wife brought a sword and called the guards. Workmen who were building a bullring in the plaza at the time joined in the fight. At least one Ute leader, Panacilla, was killed before the mayhem ended.

American Territory: 1846–1909

When Manuel Armijo returned to the palace for his third term as governor, the United States Army of the West, led by General Stephen Watts Kearny, was marching from Missouri toward Santa Fe. The troops occupied the city in August 1846. The triumphant Kearny slept on the floor of the palace the first night of occupation.

In 1846, the building was about 350 feet long on the plaza side, or about twenty-five percent longer than it is now, so it must have stretched westward almost to the sidewalk at the corner of the Museum of Fine Arts.

The principal door to the governor's residence was probably centered in the face of the building. Traditionally, Spanish architecture was symmetrical. This door is no longer in the center because the building has been shortened

Old Adobe Palace Santa Fe   Wittick Photo

The palace as recorded in the 1880s by photographer Ben Wittick.

at the west end, but it is in line with the central monument in the plaza. At the patio end of the corresponding entrance hall, Victorian woodwork was built to fit the angles of an ancient, slanting lintel. Philip St. George Cooke, on a spying mission just before the Americans entered in 1846, described the governor's carpeted earth floor, and several visitors mentioned spacious rooms with lofty ceilings.

The west end of the building was occupied by the ruined colonial jail. Its few small windows were grated and may have had wooden shutters.

Interior hallway of the palace, 1893.

Some of the small, old windows in the palace were probably glazed with selenite (a translucent stone) or thick sheets of mica. Evidence of this type of window was found during renovation in the mid-1970s. When the American army arrived in 1846, Santa Fe's only glass windows faced the plaza from the palace. In June of that year, Alfred S. Waugh, an artist, wrote that the windows in the palace were large, although the doors were not, and at least part of the building was whitewashed.

After Kearny's arrival, the U.S. Army took over the old presidio and remodeled some of the buildings to suit its needs, claiming the area as federal property. In the palace, several rooms were "fitted up" to accommodate both houses of the legislature. One of the larger rooms, which had been used for fandangos, was later converted into a theater under the auspices of Governor Charles Bent in 1846.

In the spring of 1982, an archaeological investigation of the area north of the palace, now covered by the First Interstate Bank Building, revealed Spanish-period structures from the presidio which had been remodeled and used by the Americans. In the area of the dig, the Spanish buildings were first adapted into a commissary storehouse. About 1859, these buildings were again remodeled, this time into a carpenter's work area and blacksmith shop.

The palace rooms soon contained the offices and archives of the governor and secretary of the treasury, as well as the legislature. Some of the government's most valuable weapons were also stored there. About this time the first American-style portal of sawn wood replaced the Spanish-style portal. Some Americans considered the local adobe architecture barbaric and were quick to update it with a simplified neoclassical style. The first American portal at the palace had a plain cornice over squared wooden columns. Sawn lumber characterized the trendy new territorial style.

In 1861, the government carpenter and blacksmith shops burned. When the fire threatened to spread to the palace and the post office, which seems to have replaced the government printing office, a building in between was pulled down, forming a successful firebreak.

During Governor David Meriwether's term in the 1850s, construction began on a fine, stone government building and a jail in the north area of the old presidio. Although the buildings remained roofless and unfinished for many years, the Americans connected the government building to the plaza with a wide street. This route went through part of the old *casas reales* jail. The jail end was certainly in miserable condition by that time. We do not know for certain what other rooms in that end of the palace were removed, but one of these rooms may have been used to host visiting Indians or for making treaties. We do know that some twenty years after Santa Fe became a United States territory, about a quarter of the palace was removed to make way for Lincoln Street, which led to the stone building—eventually completed as the Federal Courthouse.

As the structure of the government became more complex, ownership of the palace was divided to meet new needs. The federal government built a vault in the west end, an area that at various times housed the House of Representatives, the Office of Indian Affairs, the U.S. Depository (1869–76), the Receiver of the U.S. Land Office, the Office of the U.S. Marshall and the U.S. Attorney (1882), and the Second National Bank. By 1883, it was the site of the post office. The central section was traditionally used by the governor for his office and home. In the 1850s the east end was described as being in ruins. It seems to have been remodeled in 1867 into two long, adjoining rooms to house the legislature. These rooms were also used for public meetings. Nearby, a room was repaired to house the Territorial Library, and a series of rooms between the library and the governor's apartments were used as offices. The rights to these offices were sometimes hotly contested between the governor, the territorial secretary, and others.

A series of ever more elaborate porches replaced the portal, and each bureaucratic entity vied for attention with turnings, spindles, and balustered railings. In 1877 a large brick cornice was added to the east end, matching moulded brick chimneys were built, and the outside of the palace was plastered with white lime and sand with imitation stone blocks painted on it.

Interior of the U.S. Post Office in the palace, circa 1894–96.

Ben Hur Room.

Each tenant complained of the cost of upkeep on the old structure. Cotton sheeting was tacked to the vigas to catch the dirt sifting down from the roof. Worse, the vigas began to rot and sag, and the occupants sometimes feared for their lives. Of one such room, Governor Lew Wallace wrote, "the cedar rafters, rain-stained as those in the dining-hall of Cedric the Saxon, and overweighted by tons and tons of mud . . . had the threatening downward curvature of a shipmate's cutlass. Nevertheless, in that cavernous chamber I wrote the eighth and last book of Ben-Hur." After the book's tremendous success, the room became known as "the Ben Hur Room."

Technically, the palace was the property of the U.S. Department of the Interior, but in 1898 Congress "donated" it to the territory of New Mexico. The seemingly unending need for repairs had a strong influence on the donation. Governor Miguel Antonio Otero was hardly enthusiastic about the gift but urged that it be accepted and repaired.

Once under the ownership of New Mexico, the palace was offered to the Smithsonian Institution as a western branch of the national museum. Exciting new finds of prehistoric ruins in the southwest, such as those found by Edgar Lee Hewett at Puye and the Pajarito Plateau, had stirred national interest in archaeology. Hewett had begun to work at the Smithsonian in 1904. Theodore Roosevelt may have been the sole member of the Smithsonian's board in favor of acquiring the building or who understood its historical significance. In any event, when he assumed the presidency and left the board of the Smithsonian, the idea died. There was talk of selling the property for the value of the real estate, but a few people, such as former Governor L. Bradford Prince and Hewett, recognized the historical value of the ancient building.

The Palace in the Twentieth Century

Finally, in 1909, the New Mexico legislature established the Museum of New Mexico under the School of American Archaeology, later to become the School of American Research, and turned the responsibility of maintaining the building over to that organization as its permanent headquarters. The New Mexico Historical Society, headed by Prince, was already using the east end of the palace, and the legislature intended the two organizations to share the building as neighbors. However, the arrangement stipulated that the School would repair the entire building, giving it a large stake in the future of the palace. Eventually the Historical Society moved out, and the whole building came under the supervision of Edgar Lee Hewett, who had directed the School since its founding in 1907.

One of Hewett's protégés, Jesse Nusbaum, accepted the huge task of remodeling the palace. During repair of a wall near the area of the building in which archaeologists would later find the buried storage pits, he discovered a column and corbel embedded in an adobe wall. Later studies identified this feature as one of a series of old portals in that area. Nusbaum used the column and its corbel as the prototype for a replacement portal on the plaza side of the building in the process of eliminating the Victorian gingerbread and returning the palace to its Spanish-Pueblo style. Some of the changes were so successful that a new school of architecture, which would become known as "the Santa Fe style," was influenced by the design. The new facade was completed in 1913.

Today the palace generally retains the style it assumed under Nusbaum's direction. Interior rooms have been changed over the years, but they still follow the old Spanish plan of rooms surrounding a patio. In the mid-1970s a room was restored, with murals by Carl Lotave, to look much as it had early in the twentieth century under Hewett's direction. Showcases again displayed pieces of prehistoric pottery, and the ceiling was restored with great beams and inverted Indian bowls in the corners. This room commemorates Hewett's long guidance of the Museum of New Mexico and the School of American Research in the palace until the institutions were split off by the legislature in 1959 and the School moved to new quarters.

An award-winning restoration of the building under the direction of architect John Conron was completed during the 1980s. The entire roof, some of it dating back a hundred years, was replaced. New heating, ventilation, and

San Ildefonso potter Maria Martinez in the patio of the palace.

Rough Riders giving oath of allegiance in front of the palace.

security systems were installed within a roof and chimneys that faithfully replicated the former design. Provision was made for a fire-suppressant system to protect the irreplaceable building and its contents, with the hope that funding will become available to install it. When the exterior was restuccoed, the old surface revealed the plaster lined to simulate stone of the Victorian period, and sections were framed by glass panels for display.

The remarkable old palace continues to unveil its secrets. It represents the Indian heritage from prehistoric times to the present, as Pueblo Indians continue to sell handmade wares under its wide portal. It recalls the might of the Spanish Empire in its very form—the strong adobe walls that protected those who brought their books, laws, religion, and technology from Mexico and distant Europe. In front of the palace, Melgares proudly raised the Mexican flag. From here, expeditions began and ended, until the name "Santa Fe" came to mean the ultimate limit of the frontier to Americans. As the home of the School of American Research for many years, the palace contributed to the study of the past cultural riches of the Southwest. Today, the Palace of the Governors continues to offer the rich experience of former times to visitors of this ancient and remarkable place.

This essay is based on "The Museum's Adobe Palace" by Carrie Forman Arnold, which appeared in El Palacio 90, no. 2 (1984): 36-45.

Firewood vendor on Palace Avenue, circa 1911.

Suggested Reading

References to Santa Fe appear in countless books on the history of New Mexico and the Southwest; however, few books focus on the history of Santa Fe itself, and most sources are highly specific or scholarly. Two good resources for researchers are the Museum of New Mexico's History Library and the New Mexico State Records Center and Archives, both in Santa Fe. The *New Mexico Historical Review* and *El Palacio* are periodicals recommended for the multitude of articles they contain on specialized topics relating to Santa Fe history. Persons seeking archaeological data may wish to refer to the Arroyo Hondo Archaeological Series, published by the School of American Research Press. The following titles, which do not include technical or esoteric literature, will help readers pursue further studies on the subject.

Adams, Eleanor B., and Fray Angelico Chávez.
The Missions of New Mexico, 1776: A Description of Fray Francisco Atanacio Dominguez with Other Contemporary Documents. Albuquerque: University of New Mexico Press, 1956.

Drumm, Stella M., ed.
Down the Santa Fe Trail and into Mexico: The Diary of Susan Shelby Magoffin, 1846–1847. Lincoln, Nebraska: University of Nebraska Press, 1982.

Espinosa, J. Manuel.
First Expedition of Vargas into New Mexico, 1692. Albuquerque: University of New Mexico Press, 1940.

Hackett, Charles Wilson, ed., and Charmion Clair Shelby, trans.
Revolt of the Pueblo Indians of New Mexico and Otermin's Attempted Reconquest 1680–1682. Albuquerque: University of New Mexico Press, 1942.

Hazen-Hammond, Susan.
A Short History of Santa Fe. Lexicos, 1988.

Horgan, Paul.
The Centuries of Santa Fe. Santa Fe: William Gannon, 1976.

La Farge, Oliver, and Arthur N. Morgan.
Santa Fe: The Autobiography of a Southwestern Town. Norman, Oklahoma: University of Oklahoma Press, 1959.

Simmons, Marc.
Yesterday in Santa Fe. San Marcos Press, 1969.

Twitchell, Ralph Emerson.
Old Santa Fe: The Story of New Mexico's Ancient Capital. Chicago: Rio Grande Press, 1963. Originally published in 1925.

Picture Credits

Abbreviations: AN artifact number; LA-MNM Laboratory of Anthropology, Museum of New Mexico; NN negative number; PA-MNM Photo Archives, Museum of New Mexico; PGM-MNM Palace of the Governors Museum, Museum of New Mexico; SAR School of American Research.

Page *ix:* PA-MNM (NN10110). *xii:* PA-MNM (NN23306). 2: photo by Rod Hook. 3: photos by Rod Hook. 4: LA-MNM. 5: from *The Undeveloped West. . .*, John H. Beadle, Philadelphia, 1873. PA-MNM (NN144637) 7: PA-MNM (NN51395), photo by T. Harmon Parkhurst. 8: LA-MNM. 9: collections LA-MNM (AN17646), photo by Rod Hook. 10 top: From *Bandelier National Monument,* David Grant Noble, SAR, Santa Fe, 1980, drawing by Richard W. Lang. 10 bottom: collections LA-MNM (AN43863), photo by Rod Hook. 11 top: collections LA-MNM (AN19509), photo by Rod Hook. 11 bottom: photo by David Noble. 12: PA-MNM (NN31328). 13: PA-MNM (NN61150), photo by Valle de Vano. 14: drawing by Richard W. Lang. 15: LA-MNM archaeological site records. 16: LA-MNM. 17: photo by David Grant Noble. 18 top: SAR, photo by David Noble. 18 bottom: SAR, photo by David Noble. 19: SAR, photo by A. Stoker. 20 top: collections of the LA-MNM. 20 bottom: collections of the LA-MNM (AN47026), photo by Rod Hook. 21: PA-MNM (NN6821), photo by Arthur Taylor. 22: LA-MNM. 23 top: collection of David Snow, photo by Rod Hook. 23 bottom: collection of the LA-MNM (AN1955), photo by Rod Hook. 24: PA-MNM (NN12227), photo by Aaron B. Craycraft. 28: from Harpers Weekly, September 13, 1879. PA-MNM (NN133403). 29: PA-MNM (NN145015). 30: Special Collections, General Library, University of New Mexico. 31: from

The Story of New Mexico, Horatio Ladd, Boston, 1891. PA-MNM (NN133133). 32: collections PGM-MNM, PA-MNM (NN51249), photo by Ken Schar. 33: collections SAR, photo by Deborah Flynn. 34: photo by Karl Kernberger. 36: PA-MNM (NN82387), photo by M. C. Stevenson. 37: from *Kiva, Cross, and Crown,* John L. Kessell, Washington, D. C., 1979. 39: poster by Parker Boyiddle, courtesy Alfonso Ortiz. 40: from *Official Report of the Territory of New Mexico,* William Ritch, Santa Fe, 1882-83. PA-MNM (NN133140) 41: from *The Marvelous Country,* Samuel W. Cozzens, Boston, 1876. PA-MNM (NN133131). 43: PA-MNM (NN135333). 44: photo by Karl Kernberger. 45: collections of PGM-MNM, PA-MNM (NN505), photo by Wyatt Davis. 46: map by Katrina Lasko, adapted from "Pueblos Abandoned in Historic Times," Handbook of North American Indians, Vol. 9, Albert H. Schroeder, Washington, D. C., 1979. 48: from Official Report of the Territory of New Mexico, William Ritch, Santa Fe, 1882-83. PA-MNM (NN89210) 50: PA-MNM (NN11047), photo by T. Harmon Parkhurst. 51: Rod Hook, photo by H. C. Tibbetts. 53: PA-MNM (NN11409). 54: Bureau of Ethnology 55: Pecos National Monument (NN841). 56: PA-MNM (NN73815). 57: collections of the Albuquerque Museum, photo by Rod Hook. 58: collections PGM-MNM, PA-MNM (NN5736), photo by Wyatt Davis. 60: PA-MNM (NN2796), lithograph by R. H. Kern, 1847. 62: PA-MNM

(NN47997). 64: postcard from 18th-century painting at Museo de America, Madrid, Spain, courtesy Adrian Bustamante. 66: PA-MNM (NN11330). 67: PA-MNM (NN15048). 68: PA-MNM (NN11826). 69: PA-MNM (NN12583). 70: PA-MNM (NN71218), photo by Ed Andrews. 71: see p. 64 credit. 72: photo by David Noble. 73: see p. 64 credit. 75: painting by Wilson Hurley, 36"x30", collection of Albert G. Simms II. 76: PGM-MNM. 78: PA-MNM (NN76034), photo by J. R. Riddle. 80: PA-MNM (NN11645), courtesy Ernest Knee family, photo by Ernest Knee. 81: Amon Carter Museum, Fort Worth. 82: from *The Undeveloped West . . .*, John H. Beadle, Philadelphia, 1873, PA-MNM (NN144638). 83: Amon Carter Museum, adapted from *Narrative of the Texas Santa Fe Expedition,* Vol. II, George Wilkins Kendall, Harpers Bros., New York, 1844. 85: PA-MNM (NN11354), photo by William H. Jackson. 86: from *Century,* January, 1889, PA-MNM (NN144634). 87: PA-MNM (NN50809). 88: PA-MNM (NN13140). 89: PA-MNM (NN125551). 90: from *Harpers,* April, 1880, PA-MNM (NN133247). 91: from *Harpers,* April, 1854, PA-MNM (NN50815). 93: PA-MNM (NN36391), photo by Ina Sizer Cassidy. 94: PA-MNM (NN11070), photo by Christian G. Kaadt. 98: PA-MNM (NN7605), engraving by T. B. Welch (from a daguerreotype). 99: collections PGM-MNM, photo by Rod Hook. 100: from *Harpers,* New York, July, 1880, PA-MNM (NN133221). 101: PA-MNM (NN101912), map by J. F.

Gilmore. 102: PA-MNM (NN7174), photo by Bennett and Brown. 103: Amon Carter Museum, woodcut based on drawing by L. A. Maclean in *Doniphan's Expedition* by John T. Hughes (Cincinnati, 1847) 104: PA-MNM (NN10310). 105: PA-MNM (NN1727). 106: map by Katrina Lasko. 107: collections PGM-MNM, photo by Rod Hook. 108: from *Aztlan,* William Ritch, Boston, 1885, PA-MNM (NN10672). 109: PA-MNM (NN103021), photo by Nicholas Brown. 110: PA-MNM (NN11405). 111: PA-MNM (NN1725), photo by H. H. Dorman. 112: PA-MNM (NN50323). 113: PA-MNM (NN7004). 114: from *The Commerce of the Prairies,* Josiah Gregg. Denver Public Library Western Collection. 116: from *Massacres of the Mountains,* J. P. Dunn, Jr., New York, 1886, PA-MNM (NN7757). 118: PA-MNM (NN11329). 119: from *Harper's,* New York, July, 1880, PA-MNM (NN71387). 120: map by Katrina Lasko. 121: Kansas Collection, University of Kansas Libraries. 122: PA-MNM (NN11254). 123: PA-MNM (NN1706). 124: PA-MNM (NN11954). 125: collections Fine Arts Museum-MNM, oil on canvas, 36¼"x60½" 126: PA-MNM (NN30824). 126: collections Fine Arts Museum-MNM, PA-MNM (NN37916). 127: SAR collections at the PA-MNM (NN15870), photo by Ben Wittick. 128: PA-MNM (NN45819), photo by Nicholas Brown. 130 top: LA-MNM archaeological site records. 130 bottom: collections PGM-MNM, photo by Rod Hook. 131: PA-MNM (NN40929). 132, 133: LA-MNM archaeological site records. 135: photo by Paul Logsdon, overlay by Katrina Lasko from information supplied by Carrie Forman Arnold. 137: PGM-MNM. 139: from *Marvels of the New West,* William Thayer, Norwich, Connecticut, 1888, PA-MNM (NN11212). 141: SAR collections at the PA-MNM (NN15376). Photo by Ben Wittick. 142: PA-MNM (NN46776). Photo by Thomas J. Curran. 143: PA-MNM (NN16659), photo by Adolph Fischer. 144: PA-MNM (NN12175). 145: PA-MNM (NN42317). 146: PA-MNM (NN5989). 147: PA-MNM (NN16731).

Index